National Industrial Security Program Operating Manual (NISPOM)

DoD 5220.22-M
Incorporating Change 2
May 18, 2016

For more information on NISPOM, books, training and security, see our video @
www.redbikepublishing.com/security

National Industrial Security Program Operating Manual
(NISPOM)
DoD 5220.22-M
Incorporating Change 2
May 18, 2016

www.redbikepublishing.com

National Industrial Security Program Operating Manual (NISPOM) Incorporating Change 2 May 18, 2016

Published by: Red Bike Publishing

Published in the United States of America

www.redbikepublishing.com

ISBN-13: 9780981620657

DoD 5220.22-M

National Industrial Security Program

Operating Manual

February 2006

Incorporating Change 2,
May 18, 2016

TABLE OF CONTENTS

Page

Table of Contents 2

References 12

AL1. Acronyms 15

CHAPTER 1. GENERAL PROVISIONS AND REQUIREMENTS

Section 1. Introduction
    1-100. Purpose 1-1-1
    1-101. Authority...1-1-1
    1-102. Scope...1-1-2
    1-103. Agency Agreements 1-1-2
    1-104. Security Cognizance 1-1-2
    1-105. Composition of Manual..1-1-3
    1-106. Manual Interpretations...1-1-3
    1-107. Waivers and Exceptions to this Manual 1-1-3
    1-108. Releasability and Effective Date 1-1-3
Section 2. General Requirements
    1-200. General..1-2-1
    1-201. Facility Security Officer (FSO)..1-2-1
    1-202. Insider Threat Program 1-2-1
    1-203. Standard Practice Procedures...1-2-1
    1-204. One-Person Facilities 1-2-1
    1-205. Cooperation with Federal Agencies and Officially Credentialed
    Representatives of Those Agencies 1-2-1
    1-206. Security Training and Briefings..1-2-1
    1-207. Security Reviews 1-2-1
    1-208. Hotlines..1-2-2
    1-209. Classified Information Procedures Act (CIPA)........................1-2-2
Section 3. Reporting Requirements
    1-300. General..1-3-1
    1-301. Reports to be Submitted to the FBI 1-3-1
    1-302. Reports to be Submitted to the CSA...1-3-2
    1-303. Reports of Loss, Compromise, or Suspected Compromise 1-3-2
    1-304. Individual Culpability Reports...1-3-3
Section 4. Reports to DoD About Cyber Incidents On Cleared Defense Contractors (CDCs) ISs
Approved to Process Classified Information
    1-400. General..1-4-1
    1-401. Reports to be Submitted to DoD...1-4-1
    1-402. Access to Equipment and Information by DoD Personnel..................1-4-1

CHAPTER 2. SECURITY CLEARANCES

Section 1. Facility Clearances
2-100. General..2-1-1
2-101. Reciprocity 2-1-1
2-102. Eligibility Requirements...2-1-1
2-103. Processing the FCL...2-1-1
2-104. PCLs Required in Connection with the FCL 2-1-1
2-105. PCLs Concurrent with the FCL 2-1-1
2-106. Exclusion Procedures 2-1-1
2-107. Interim FCLs 2-1-2
2-108. Multiple Facility Organizations (MFOs)..2-1-2
2-109. Parent-Subsidiary Relationships 2-1-2
2-110. Termination of the FCL...2-1-2
2-111. Records Maintenance 2-1-2
Section 2. Personnel Security Clearances
2-200. General..2-2-1
2-201. Investigative Requirements 2-2-1
2-202. Procedures for Completing the Electronic Version of the SF 86 2-2-1
2-203. Common Adjudicative Standards..2-2-2
2-204. Reciprocity 2-2-2
2-205. Pre-employment Clearance Action...2-2-2
2-206. Contractor-Granted Clearances...2-2-2
2-207. Verification of U.S. Citizenship 2-2-2
2-208. Acceptable Proof of Citizenship 2-2-2
2-209. Non-U.S. Citizens 2-2-3
2-210. Access Limitations of an LAA 2-2-3
2-211. Interim PCLs 2-2-3
2-212. Consultants 2-2-3
Section 3. Foreign Ownership, Control, or Influence (FOCI)
2-300. Policy..2-3-1
2-301. Factors...2-3-1
2-302. Procedures 2-3-2
2-303. FOCI Action Plans 2-3-2
2-304. Citizenship of Persons Requiring PCLs 2-3-3
2-305. Qualifications of Trustees, Proxy Holders, and Outside Directors 2-3-4
2-306. GSC...2-3-4
2-307. TCP 2-3-4
2-308. Annual Review and Certification 2-3-4
2-309. Limited FCL...2-3-5
2-310. Foreign Mergers, Acquisitions and Takeovers and the Committee on
Foreign Investment in the United States (CFIUS)...............................2-3-5

CHAPTER 3. SECURITY TRAINING AND BRIEFINGS

Section 1. Security Training and Briefings
  3-100. General...3-1-1
  3-101. Training Materials...3-1-1
  3-102. FSO Training..3-1-1
  3-103. Insider Threat Training 3-1-1
  3-104. Government-Provided Briefings...3-1-1
  3-105. Temporary Help Suppliers 3-1-1
  3-106. Classified Information Nondisclosure Agreement (SF 312) 3-1-1
  3-107. Initial Security Briefings...3-1-2
  3-108. Refresher Training 3-1-2
  3-109. Debriefings 3-1-2

CHAPTER 4. CLASSIFICATION AND MARKING

Section 1. Classification
  4-100. General 4-1-1
  4-101. Original Classification..4-1-1
  4-102. Derivative Classification Responsibilities...................................4-1-1
  4-103. Security Classification Guidance 4-1-2
  4-104. Challenges to Classification...4-1-2
  4-105. Contractor Developed Information 4-1-2
  4-106. Classified Information Appearing in Public Media..........................4-1-3
  4-107. Downgrading or Declassifying Classified Information 4-1-3
Section 2. Marking Requirements
  4-200. General...4-2-1
  4-201. Marking Requirements for Information and Material.......................4-2-1
  4-202. Identification Markings 4-2-1
  4-203. Overall Markings 4-2-1
  4-204. Page Markings..4-2-1
  4-205. Component Markings 4-2-1
  4-206. Portion Markings 4-2-1
  4-207. Subject and Title Markings 4-2-2
  4-208. Markings for Derivatively Classified Documents 4-2-2
  4-209. Documents Generated Under Previous E.O.s.................................4-2-2
  4-210. Marking Special Types of Material 4-2-3
  4-211. Marking Transmittal Documents...4-2-3
  4-212. Marking Wholly Unclassified Material..4-2-3
  4-213. Marking Compilations...4-2-4
  4-214. Working Papers..4-2-4
  4-215. Marking Miscellaneous Material..4-2-4
  4-216. Marking Training Material..4-2-4
  4-217. Downgrading or Declassification Actions 4-2-4
  4-218. Upgrading Action 4-2-4
  4-219. Inadvertent Release..4-2-5
  4-220. Marking requirements for transfers of defense articles to AUS or the

UK..4-2-5
4-221. Comingling of Restricted Data (RD) and Formerly Restricted
Data (FRD)..4-2-5

CHAPTER 5. SAFEGUARDING CLASSIFIED INFORMATION

Section 1. General Safeguarding Requirements
    5-100. General...5-1-1
    5-101. Safeguarding Oral Discussions...5-1-1
    5-102. End of Day Security Checks...5-1-1
    5-103. Perimeter Controls..5-1-1
    5-104. Emergency Procedures..5-1-1

Section 2. Control and Accountability
    5-200. Policy..5-2-1
    5-201. Accountability for TOP SECRET..5-2-1
    5-202. Receiving Classified Material..5-2-1
    5-203. Generation of Classified Material..5-2-1
Section 3. Storage and Storage Equipment
    5-300. General..5-3-1
    5-301. GSA Storage Equipment...5-3-1
    5-302. TOP SECRET Storage...5-3-1
    5-303. SECRET Storage...5-3-1
    5-304. CONFIDENTIAL Storage..5-3-1
    5-305. Restricted Areas...5-3-1
    5-306. Closed Areas...5-3-1
    5-307. Supplemental Protection...5-3-2
    5-308. Protection of Combinations to Security Containers, Cabinets, Vaults
    and Closed Areas 5-3-2
    5-309. Changing Combinations...5-3-2
    5-310. Supervision of Keys and Padlocks...5-3-2
    5-311. Repair of Approved Containers...5-3-2
    5-312. Supplanting Access Control Systems or Devices 5-3-3
    5-313. Automated Access Control Systems..5-3-3
    5-314. Electronic, Mechanical, or Electro-mechanical Devices............5-3-4
Section 4. Transmission
    5-400. General..5-4-1
    5-401. Preparation and Receipting 5-4-1
    5-402. TOP SECRET Transmission Outside a Facility.........................5-4-1
    5-403. SECRET Transmission Outside a Facility.................................5-4-1
    5-404. CONFIDENTIAL Transmission Outside a Facility 5-4-1
    5-405. Transmission Outside the United States and Its Territorial Areas........5-4-1
    5-406. Addressing Classified Material...5-4-2
    5-407. Transmission Within a Facility...5-4-2
    5-408. SECRET Transmission by Commercial Carrier 5-4-2
    5-409. CONFIDENTIAL Transmission by Commercial Carrier...........5-4-3

5-410. Use of Couriers, Hand Carriers, and Escorts 5-4-3
5-411. Use of Commercial Passenger Aircraft for Transmitting
Classified Material 5-4-3
5-412. Use of Escorts for Classified Shipments 5-4-4
5-413. Functions of an Escort 5-4-4
Section 5. Disclosure
    5-500. General..5-5-1
    5-501. Disclosure to Employees 5-5-1
    5-502. Disclosure to Subcontractors..5-5-1
    5-503. Disclosure between Parent and Subsidiaries..................................5-5-1
    5-504. Disclosure in an MFO 5-5-1
    5-505. Disclosure to DoD Activities 5-5-1
    5-506. Disclosure to Federal Agencies...5-5-1
    5-507. Disclosure of Classified Information to Foreign Persons..................5-5-1
    5-508. Disclosure of Export Controlled Information to Foreign Persons........5-5-1
    5-509. Disclosure to Other Contractors..5-5-1
    5-510. Disclosure of Classified Information in Connection with Litigation ...5-5-1
    5-511. Disclosure to the Public..5-5-1
Section 6. Reproduction
    5-600. General..5-6-1
    5-601. Limitations..5-6-1
    5-602. Marking Reproductions..5-6-1
    5-603. Records...5-6-1
Section 7. Disposition and Retention
    5-700. General..5-7-1
    5-701. Retention of Classified Material 5-7-1
    5-702. Termination of Security Agreement..5-7-1
    5-703. Disposition of Classified Material Not Received Under a Specific
Contract 5-7-1
    5-704. Destruction 5-7-1
    5-705. Methods of Destruction 5-7-1
    5-706. Witness to Destruction...5-7-2
    5-707. Destruction Records...5-7-2
    5-708. Classified Waste...5-7-2
Section 8. Construction Requirements
    5-800. General..5-8-1
    5-801. Construction Requirements for Closed Areas...................................5-8-1
    5-802. Construction Requirements for Vaults 5-8-2
Section 9. Intrusion Detection Systems
    5-900. General..5-9-1
    5-901. CSA Approval..5-9-1
    5-902. Central Monitoring Station..5-9-1
    5-903. Investigative Response to Alarms..5-9-1
    5-904. Installation 5-9-2
    5-905. Certification of Compliance..5-9-2
    5-906. Exceptional Cases 5-9-2

CHAPTER 6. VISITS and MEETINGS

Section 1. Visits
    6-100. General..6-1-1
    6-101. Classified Visits..6-1-1
    6-102. Need-to-Know Determination...6-1-1
    6-103. Visits by Government Representatives 6-1-1
    6-104. Visit Authorization...6-1-1
    6-105. Long-Term Visitors..6-1-1
Section 2. Meetings
    6-200. General..6-2-1
    6-201. Government Sponsorship of Meetings...6-2-1
    6-202. Disclosure Authority at Meetings...6-2-2
    6-203. Requests to Attend Classified Meetings......................................6-2-2

CHAPTER 7. SUBCONTRACTING

Section 1. Prime Contractor Responsibilities
    7-100. General..7-1-1
    7-101. Responsibilities..7-1-1
    7-102. Security Classification Guidance...7-1-1
    7-103. Responsibilities (Completion of the Subcontract)....................7-1-2
    7-104. Notification of Unsatisfactory Conditions.............................7-1-2

CHAPTER 8. IS SECURITY

Section 1. Responsibilities and Duties
    8-100. General..8-1-1
    8-101. IS Security Program..8-1-1
    8-102. System Security Plan...8-1-1
    8-103. Contractor Roles & Responsibilities..8-1-1
Section 2. Assessment and Authorization
    8-200. Overview...8-2-1
    8-201. Assessment..8-2-1
    8-202. Authorization 8-2-1
Section 3. Security Controls
    8-300. Security Controls..8-3-1
    8-301. Management Controls 8-3-1
    8-302. Operational Controls...8-3-1
    8-303. Technical Controls..8-3-3
    8-304. Special Categories...8-3-3

CHAPTER 9. SPECIAL REQUIREMENTS

Section 1. RD and FRD, and Transclassified Foreign Nuclear Information (TFNI)
    9-100. General..9-1-1

Section 2. DoD Critical Nuclear Weapon Design Information (CNWDI)
    9-200. General..9-2-1
    9-201. Background 9-2-1
    9-202. Briefings...9-2-1
    9-203. Markings...9-2-1
    9-204. Subcontractors..9-2-1
    9-205. Transmission Outside the Facility..9-2-1
    9-206. Records...9-2-1
    9-207. Weapon Data..9-2-1
Section 3. Intelligence Information
    9-300. General..9-3-1
Section 4. Communication Security (COMSEC)
    9-400. General..9-4-1
    9-401. Instructions 9-4-1
    9-402. Clearance and Access Requirements...9-4-1
    9-403. Establishing a COMSEC Account 9-4-1
    9-404. COMSEC Briefing and Debriefing Requirements..............................9-4-1
    9-405. CRYPTO Access Briefing and Debriefing Requirements 9-4-2
    9-406. Destruction and Disposition of COMSEC Material............................9-4-2
    9-407. Subcontracting COMSEC Work 9-4-2
    9-408. Unsolicited Proposals 9-4-2

CHAPTER 10. INTERNATIONAL SECURITY REQUIREMENTS

Section 1. General and Background Information
    10-100. General...10-1-1
    10-101. Applicable Federal Laws..10-1-1
    10-102. Bilateral Security Agreements..10-1-1
Section 2. Disclosure of U.S. Information to Foreign Interests
    10-200. Authorization for Disclosure 10-2-1
    10-201. Direct Commercial Arrangements...10-2-1
    10-202. Contract Security Provisions 10-2-1
Section 3. Foreign Government Information
    10-300. General...10-3-1
    10-301. Contract Security Requirements..10-3-1
    10-302. Marking Foreign Government Classified Material..............................10-3-1
    10-303. Foreign Government RESTRICTED Information and
    "In Confidence" Information 10-3-1
    10-304. Marking U.S. Documents Containing FGI...10-3-1
    10-305. Marking Documents Prepared For Foreign Governments 10-3-1
    10-306. Storage and Control 10-3-2
    10-307. Disclosure and Use Limitations..10-3-2

10-308. Transfer...10-3-2
10-309. Reproduction...10-3-2
10-310. Disposition 10-3-2
10-311. Reporting of Improper Receipt of Foreign Government Material.....10-3-2
10-312. Subcontracting..10-3-2
Section 4. International Transfers
10-400. General..10-4-1
10-401. International Transfers of Classified Material..10-4-1
10-402. Transfers of Freight..10-4-1
10-403. Return of Material for Repair, Modification, or Maintenance..........10-4-2
10-404. Use of Freight Forwarders..10-4-2
10-405. Hand Carrying Classified Material 10-4-2
10-406. Classified Material Receipts...10-4-3
10-407. Contractor Preparations for International Transfers Pursuant to
Commercial and User Agency Sales...10-4-3
10-408. Transfers Pursuant to an ITAR Exemption..10-4-3
Section 5. International Visits and Control of Foreign Nationals
10-500. General..10-5-1
10-501. International Visits..10-5-1
10-502. Types and Purpose of International Visits 10-5-1
10-503. Emergency Visits...10-5-1
10-504. Requests for Recurring Visits...10-5-1
10-505. Amendments...10-5-1
10-506. Visits Abroad by U.S. Contractors 10-5-1
10-507. Visits by Foreign Nationals to U.S. Contractor Facilities..................10-5-2
10-508. Control of Access by On-Site Foreign Nationals.................................10-5-2
10-509. TCP 10-5-3
10-510. Security and Export Control Violations Involving Foreign Nationals 10-5-3
Section 6. Contractor Operations Abroad.
10-600. General..10-6-1
10-601. Access by Contractor Employees Assigned Outside the
United States..10-6-1
10-602. Storage, Custody, and Control of Classified Information Abroad
by Employees of a U.S. Contractor...10-6-1
10-603. Transmission of Classified Material to Employees Abroad 10-6-1
10-604. Security Briefings...10-6-2
Section 7. NATO Information Security Requirements
10-700. General..10-7-1
10-701. Classification Levels...10-7-1
10-702. NATO RESTRICTED 10-7-1
10-703. NATO Contracts...10-7-1
10-704. NATO Facility Security Clearance Certificate.....................................10-7-1
10-705. PCL Requirements 10-7-1
10-706. NATO Briefings..10-7-1
10-707. Access to NATO Classified Information by Foreign Nationals..........10-7-1
10-708. Subcontracting for NATO Contracts..10-7-1

10-709. Preparing and Marking NATO Documents 10-7-1
10-710. Classification Guidance 10-7-2
10-711. Further Distribution 10-7-2
10-712. Storage of NATO Documents...10-7-2
10-713. International Transmission..10-7-2
10-714. Hand Carrying..10-7-3
10-715. Reproduction...10-7-3
10-716. Disposition..10-7-3
10-717. Accountability Records..10-7-3
10-718. Security Violations and Loss, Compromise, or Possible
Compromise 10-7-3
10-719. Extracting from NATO Documents..10-7-3
10-720. Release of U.S. Information to NATO...10-7-4
10-721. Visits..10-7-4
Section 8. Transfers of Defense Articles to AUS or the UK
without a License or Other Written Authorization....................................10-8-1
10-800. General 10-8-1
10-801. Defense Articles..10-8-1
10-802. Marking Requirements...10-8-1
10-803. Notice 10-8-1
10-804. Labelling...10-8-2
10-805. Transfers..10-8-2
10-806. Records..10-8-2

CHAPTER 11. MISCELLANEOUS INFORMATION

Section 1. TEMPEST
11-100. General..11-1-1
11-101. TEMPEST Requirements 11-1-1
11-102. Cost...11-1-1
Section 2. Defense Technical Information Center (DTIC)
11-200. General..11-2-1
11-201. User Community..11-2-1
11-202. Registration Process...11-2-1
11-203. Safeguarding Requirements...11-2-1
11-204. DTIC Downgrading or Declassification Notices 11-2-1
11-205. Questions Concerning Reference Material 11-2-1
11-206. Subcontracts..11-2-1
Section 3. Independent Research and Development (IR&D) Efforts
11-300. General..11-3-1
11-301. Information Generated Under an IR&D Effort that Incorporates

Classified Information 11-3-1

11-302. Classification Guidance..11-3-1
11-303. Preparation of Security Guidance..11-3-1
11-304. Retention of Classified Documents Generated Under IR&D Efforts11-3-1

APPENDIXES

Appendix A. Cognizant Security Office Information...A-1
Appendix B. International Visits Standard Request for Visit Format (RFV).....................B-1
Appendix C. Definitions...C-1
Appendix D. NISPOM Supplement – Security Requirements for SAPS, SCI, IC Compartmented Programs, RD and FRD D-1

REFERENCES

(a) Executive Order 12829, "National Industrial Security Program," January 6, 1993

(b) Executive Order 13526, "Classified National Security Information," December 29, 2009

(c) Section 2011 et seq. of title 42, United States Code, "Atomic Energy Act of 1954," as amended

(d) Section 403 of title 50, United States Code, "National Security Act of 1947," as amended

(e) Executive Order 12333, "United States Intelligence Activities," December 4, 1981, as amended

(f) Public Law 108-458, "Intelligence Reform and Terrorism Prevention Act of 2004," 118 Stat. 3638, December 17, 2004[1]

(g) Section 781 of title 50, United States Code, "Internal Security Act of 1950"

(h) Section 552(f) of title 5, United States Code, "Government Organization and Employees"

(i) DoD 5220.22-C, "Carrier Supplement to the Industrial Security Manual for Safeguarding Classified Information," October 1986

(j) Title 18 USC, Appendix 3, "Classified Information Procedures Act (CIPA)"

(k) Section 552 of title 5, United States Code, "Freedom of Information Act"

(l) Section 552a of title 5, United States Code, "Privacy Act of 1975"

(m) Section 2170 of Title 50, United States Code Appendix, "Defense Production Act of 1950"

(n) Intelligence Community Directive 705, "Sensitive Compartmented Information Facilities (SCIFs)," May 26, 2010.

(o) Underwriters Laboratories Standard 2050, "Standard for National Industrial Security Systems for the Protection of Classified Materials," current edition[2]

(p) Title 10, Code of Federal Regulations

(q) DoD Instruction 5210.02, "Access to and Dissemination of Restricted Data and Formerly Restricted Data," June 3, 2011

(r) Department of Energy Order 452.8, "Control of Nuclear Weapon Data," July 21, 2011

(s) Sections 793, 794, and 798 of title 18, United States Code, Chapter 37, "Espionage and Censorship"

(t) Section 2751 et seq. of title 22, United States Code, "Arms Export Control Act (AECA)," June 30, 1976, as amended

(u) App. 2401 et seq. of title 50, United States Code, "The Export Administration Act of 1979 (EAA)," September 29, 1979, as amended

(v) Title 22, Code of Federal Regulations, Parts 120-130, "International Traffic in Arms Regulations," current edition

(w) Section 130(c) of title 10, United States Code, "Authority to Withhold from Public Disclosure Certain Technical Data"

(x) Section 1101(a)(22) and Section 1401, subsection (a) of title 8, United States Code, "Aliens and Nationality"

(y) Title15, Code of Federal Regulations, parts 368.1-399.2, "Export Administration Regulation (EAR)," current edition

(z) Title 32, Code of Federal Regulations

---

[1] Not codified

[2] Copy is available at www.ul.com/contact us. Government agencies with a role as a Cognizant Security Agency or Cognizant Security Office may obtain this reference without charge.

(aa) Information Security Oversight Office Notice 2011-02, "Further Guidance and Clarification on Commingling Atomic Energy Information and Classification National Security Information," May 18, 2011

(ab) DoD 5220.22-M, Supplement 1, "National Industrial Security Program Operating Manual Supplement," February 1, 1995 (hereby cancelled)

(ac) Executive Order 13587, "Structural Reforms To Improve the Security of Classified Networks and the Responsible Sharing and Safeguarding of Classified Information", October 7, 2011

(ad) "The National Insider Threat Policy and Minimum Standards for Executive Branch Insider Threat Programs," November 21, 2012[3]

(ae) DoD Instruction 5220.22, "National Industrial Security Program (NISP)," March 18, 2011

(af) Public Law 112-239, "National Defense Authorization Act for Fiscal Year 2013," January 2, 2013

(ag) Section 391 of title 10, United States Code,"Reporting on cyber incidents with respect to networks and information systems of operationally critical contractors and certain other contractors"

(ah) Subpart 204.73 of title 48, Code of Federal Regulations, "Safeguarding Covered Defense Information and Cyber Incident Reporting"

(ai) Section 3541 et seq. of title 44, United States Code (also known as the "Federal Information Security Management Act (FISMA)")

(aj) National Institute of Standards and Technology Special Publication 800-37, "Guide for Applying the Risk Management Framework to Federal Information Systems: A Security Life Cycle Approach" February 2010, as amended[4]

(ak) Committee on National Security Systems Directive 504, "Protecting NSS from Insider Threat," February 4, 2014

(al) National Institute of Standards and Technology Special Publication 800-53, "Security and Privacy Controls for Federal Information Systems and Organizations," current edition

(am) Committee on National Security Systems Information (CNNSI) No. 1253, "Security Categorization and Control Selection for National Security Systems," March 27, 2014"

(an) Office of Management and Budget Memorandum M-14-03, "Enhancing the Security of Federal Information and Information Systems," November 18, 2013

(ao) Treaty Between the Government of the United States of America and the Government of the United Kingdom of Great Britain and Northern Ireland Concerning Defense Trade Cooperation, June 21, 2007[5]

(ap) Treaty Between the Government of the United States of America and the Government of the Australia Concerning Defense Trade Cooperation, September 5, 2007[5]

(aq) Committee on National Security Systems Instruction No. 4009, "National Information Assurance (IA) Glossary," April 26, 2010

(ar) National Security Presidential Directive-54, "Cyber Security and Monitoring," January 8, 2008

(as) Department of Energy Order 475.2B, "Identifying Classified Information," October 3, 2014

---

[3] Copy is available at http://www.ncix.gov/nittf/docs/National_Insider_Threat_Policy.pdf
[4] Copy is available at http: //csrc.nist.gov/publications/.
[5] Copy is available at http://www.pmddtc.state.gov

(at) Department of Energy Manual 205.1B, "Department of Energy Cyber Security Program," May 16, 2011, as amended

(au) Department of Energy Order 452.7, "Protection of Use Control Vulnerabilities and Designs," May 14, 2010

(av) Department of Energy Order 452.4B, "Security and Use Control of Nuclear Explosives and Nuclear Weapons," January 22, 2010

(aw) Department of Energy Order 473.3, "Protection Program Operations," June 29, 2011

(ax) Department of Energy Order 471.6, "Information Security," June 20, 2011, as amended

(ay) Department of Energy Manual 483.1-1A, "DOE Cooperative Research and Developments Agreements Manual," November 6, 2013

AL1. Acronyms

AL.1.1. ACCM		Alternative Compensatory Control Measures
AL.1.2. AECA		Arms Export Control Act
AL.1.3. AO		Authorizing Official
AL.1.4. ASC		Alarm Service Company
AL.1.5. ATD		Authorization Termination Date
AL.1.6 ATO		Authorization to Operate
AL.1.7 AUS		Australia
AL.1.8. BL		Bill of Lading
AL.1.9. C		CONFIDENTIAL
AL.1.10. CAGE		Commercial and Government Entity
AL.1.11. CAP		Controlled Access Program
AL.1.12. CFIUS		Committee on Foreign Investment in the United States
AL.1.13. CFR		Code of Federal Regulations
AL.1.14. CI		Counterintelligence
AL.1.15. CIA		Central Intelligence Agency
AL.1.16. CM		Configuration Management
AL.1.17. CNSS		Committee on National Security Systems
AL.1.18. CNWDI		Critical Nuclear Weapons Design Information
AL.1.19. COMSEC		Communications Security
AL.1.20. COR		Central Office of Record
AL.1.21. CRYPTO		Cryptographic
AL.1.22. CSA		Cognizant Security Agency
AL.1.23. CSO		Cognizant Security Office
AL.1.24. CUSR		Central United States Registry
AL.1.25. CVA		Central Verification Activity
AL.1.26. DCID		Director of Central Intelligence Directive
AL.1.27. DDTC		Directorate of Defense Trade Controls
AL.1.28. DGR		Designated Government Representative
AL.1.29. DNI		Director of National Intelligence
AL.1.30. DOD		Department of Defense
AL.1.31. DOE		Department of Energy
AL.1.32. DOJ		Department of Justice
AL.1.33. DSS		Defense Security Service
AL.1.34. DTIC		Defense Technical Information Center
AL.1.35. EAA		Export Administration Act
AL 1.36. EPA		Environmental Protection Agency
AL.1.37. FBI		Federal Bureau of Investigation
AL.1.38. FCC		Federal Communications Commission
AL.1.39. FCL		Facility (Security) Clearance
AL.1.40. FGI		Foreign Government Information
AL.1.41. FOCI		Foreign Ownership, Control or Influence
AL.1.42. FOUO		For Official Use Only
AL.1.43. FRD		Formerly Restricted Data
AL.1.44. FRS		Federal Reserve System
AL.1.45. FSCC		NATO Facility Security Clearance Certificate
AL.1.46. FSO		Facility Security Officer
AL.1.47. GAO		Government Accountability Office

AL.1.48. GCA	Government Contracting Activity
AL.1.49. GCMS	Government Contractor Monitoring Station
AL.1.50. GFE	Government Furnished Equipment
AL.1.51. GSA	General Services Administration
AL.1.52. GSC	Government Security Committee
AL.1.53. IATO	Interim Authorization to Operate
AL.1.54. IC	Intelligence Community
AL.1.55. IDS	Intrusion Detection System
AL.1.56. IFB	Invitation for Bid
AL.1.57. IR&D	Independent Research & Development
AL.1.58. IS	Information System
AL.1.59. ISs	Information Systems
AL.1.60. ISCAP	Interagency Security Classification Appeals Panel
AL.1.61. ISL	Industrial Security Letter
AL.1.62. ISOO	Information Security Oversight Office
AL.1.63. ISR	Industrial Security Representative
AL.1.64. ISSM	Information System Security Manager
AL.1.65. ISSO	Information System Security Officer
AL.1.66. ITAR	International Traffic in Arms Regulations
AL.1.67. LAA	Limited Access Authorization
AL.1.68. LAN	Local Area Network
AL.1.69. MFO	Multiple Facility Organization
AL.1.70. NACLC	National Agency Check with Local Agency Check and Credit Check
AL.1.71. NASA	National Aeronautics and Space Administration
AL.1.72. NATO	North Atlantic Treaty Organization
AL.1.73. NIAG	NATO Industrial Advisory Group
AL.1.74. NID	National Interest Determination
AL.1.75. NISP	National Industrial Security Program
AL.1.76. NISPOM	National Industrial Security Program Operating Manual
AL.1.77. NISPOMSUP	National Industrial Security Program Operating Manual Supplement
AL.1.78. NIST	National Institute for Standards and Technology
AL.1.79. NOFORN	Not Releasable to Foreign Nationals
AL.1.80. NPLO	NATO Production Logistics Organization
AL.1.81. NRC	Nuclear Regulatory Commission
AL.1.82. NSA	National Security Agency
AL.1.83. NSF	National Science Foundation
AL.1.84. NSI	National Security Information
AL.1.85. OADR	Originating Agency's Determination Required
AL.1.86. ORCON	Dissemination and Extraction of Information Controlled by Originator
AL.1.87 PCL	Personnel (Security) Clearance
AL.1.88. PROPIN	Proprietary Information Involved
AL.1.89. RD	Restricted Data
AL.1.90. RDT&E	Research, Development, Test, and Evaluation
AL.1.91. REL TO	Authorized for Release to
AL.1.92. RFP	Request for Proposal
AL.1.93. RFQ	Request for Quotation
AL.1.94. RFV	Request for Visit
AL.1.95. S	SECRET
AL.1.96. SAP	Special Access Program

AL.1.97. SBA	Small Business Administration
AL.1.98. SCA	Security Control Agreement
AL.1.99. SCI	Sensitive Compartmented Information
AL.1.100. SCIF	Sensitive Compartmented Information Facility
AL.1.101. SDDC	Surface Deployment and Distribution Command
AL.1.102. SIO	Senior Intelligence Officer
AL.1.103. SSA	Special Security Agreement
AL.1.104. SSBI	Single Scope Background Investigation
AL.1.105. SSP	Systems Security Plan
AL.1.106. TS	TOP SECRET
AL.1.107. TCO	Technology Control Officer
AL.1.108. TCP	Technology Control Plan
AL.1.109. TFNI	Transclassified Foreign Nuclear Information
AL.1.110. TP	Transportation Plan
AL.1.111. UK	United Kingdom
AL.1.112. UL	Underwriters' Laboratories
AL.1.113. USAID	United States Agency for International Development
AL.1.114. USC	United States Code
AL.1.115. USCIS	United States Citizenship and Immigration Services
AL.1.116. USITC	United States International Trade Commission
AL.1.117. USML	United States Munitions List
AL.1.118. USTR	United States Trade Representative
AL.1.119. VAL	Visit Authorization Letter

CHAPTER 1
General Provisions and Requirements

Section 1. Introduction

1-100. Purpose. This Manual:

a. Is issued in accordance with the National Industrial Security Program (NISP). It prescribes the requirements, restrictions, and other safeguards to prevent unauthorized disclosure of classified information. The Manual controls the authorized disclosure of classified information released by U.S. Government Executive Branch Departments and Agencies to their contractors. It also prescribes the procedures, requirements, restrictions, and other safeguards to protect special classes of classified information, including Restricted Data (RD), Formerly Restricted Data (FRD), intelligence sources and methods information, Sensitive Compartmented Information (SCI), and Special Access Program (SAP) information. These procedures are applicable to licensees, grantees, and certificate holders to the extent legally and practically possible within the constraints of applicable law and the Code of Federal Regulations (CFR).

b. Incorporates and cancels DoD 5220.22-M, Supplement 1 (reference (ab)).

1-101. Authority

a. The NISP was established by Executive Order (E.O.) 12829 (reference (a)) for the protection of information classified under E.O. 13526 (reference (b)), or its successor or predecessor orders, and the Atomic Energy Act of 1954, as amended (reference (c)). The National Security Council is responsible for providing overall policy direction for the NISP. The Secretary of Defense has been designated Executive Agent for the NISP by the President. The Director, Information Security Oversight Office (ISOO), is responsible for implementing and monitoring the NISP and for issuing implementing directives that shall be binding on agencies.

b. The Secretary of Defense, in consultation with all affected agencies and with the concurrence of the Secretary of Energy, the Chairman of the Nuclear Regulatory Commission (NRC) and the Director of National Intelligence (DNI) is responsible for the issuance and maintenance of this Manual.

(1) The Secretary of Energy and the Chairman of the NRC are responsible for prescribing that portion of the Manual that pertains to information classified under reference (c). Additionally, the Secretary of Energy and the Chairman of the NRC retain authority over access to information under their respective programs classified under reference (c), and may inspect and monitor contractor, licensee, certificate holder, and grantee programs and facilities that involve access to such information.

(2) The DNI is responsible for prescribing that portion of the Manual that pertains to intelligence sources and methods, including SCI. The DNI retains authority over access to intelligence sources and methods, including SCI. The DNI's responsibilities are derived from the National Security Act of 1947, as amended (reference (d)); Executive Order (EO) 12333, as amended (reference (e)); reference (b); and The Intelligence Reform and Terrorism Prevention Act (IRTPA) of 2004 (reference (f)). For purposes of this Manual, the DNI may inspect and monitor contractor, licensee, and grantee programs and facilities that involve access to such information.

c. The Secretary of Defense serves as Executive Agent for inspecting and monitoring contractors, licensees, grantees, and certificate holders who require or will require access to, or who store or will store classified information; and for determining the eligibility for access to classified information of contractors, licensees, certificate holders, and grantees and their respective employees.

d. The Director, ISOO, will consider and take action on complaints and suggestions from persons within or outside the Government with respect to the administration of the NISP.

e. Nothing in this Manual shall be construed to supersede the authority of the Secretary of Energy or the Chairman of the NRC under reference (c). Nor shall this information detract from the authority of installation commanders under the Internal Security Act of 1950 (reference (g)); or the authority of the

DNI under reference (f). This Manual shall not detract from the authority of other applicable provisions of law, or the authority of any other Federal department or agency head granted according to U.S. statute or Presidential decree.

1-102. Scope

a. The NISP applies to all Executive Branch Departments and Agencies and to all cleared contractor facilities located within the United States and its territories.

b. This Manual applies to and shall be used by contractors to safeguard classified information released during all phases of the contracting, licensing, and grant process, including bidding, negotiation, award, performance, and termination. It also applies to classified information not released under a contract, license, certificate or grant, and to foreign government information furnished to contractors that requires protection in the interest of national security. This Manual implements applicable Federal statutes, E.O.s, national directives, international treaties, and certain government-to-government agreements.

c. Implementation of changes to this Manual by contractors shall be effected no later than 6 months from the date of the published change, with the exception of changes related to US-UK and US-Australia (AUS) Treaty requirements, in Chapters 4 and 10, Section 8 of this Manual, which must be implemented immediately.

d. This Manual does not contain protection requirements for Special Nuclear Material.

1-103. Agency Agreements

a. Reference (a) requires the Heads of Agencies to enter into agreements with the Secretary of Defense as the Executive Agent for the NISP. This is designated by Presidential guidance that establishes the terms of the Secretary's responsibilities on behalf of these agency heads.

b. The Secretary of Defense has entered into agreements with the departments and agencies listed below for the purpose of rendering industrial security services. This delegation of authority is contained in an exchange of letters between the Secretary of Defense and (1) the Administrator, National Aeronautics and Space Administration (NASA); (2) the Secretary of Commerce; (3) the Administrator, General Services Administration (GSA); (4) the Secretary of State; (5) the Administrator, Small Business Administration (SBA); (6) the Director, National Science Foundation (NSF); (7) the Secretary of the Treasury; (8) the Secretary of Transportation; (9) the Secretary of the Interior; (10) the Secretary of Agriculture; (11) the Secretary of Labor; (12) the Administrator, Environmental Protection Agency (EPA); (13) the Attorney General, Department of Justice (DOJ); (14) the Chairman, Board of Governors, Federal Reserve System (FRS); (15) the Comptroller General of the United States, Government Accountability Office (GAO); (16) the Director of Administrative Services, United States Trade Representative (USTR); (17) the Director of Administration, United States International Trade Commission (USITC); (18) the Administrator, United States Agency for International Development (USAID); (19) the Executive Director for Operations of the NRC; (20) the Secretary of Education; (21) the Secretary of Health and Human Services; (22) the Secretary of Homeland Security; (23) the Deputy Managing Director, Federal Communications Commission (FCC); (24) the Deputy Director, Facilities, Security, and Contracting, Office of Personnel Management; (25) the Archivist, United States National Archives and Records Administration; (26) the President and Chief Executive Officer, Overseas Private Investment Corporation; (27) the Deputy Secretary, Department of Housing and Urban Development; (28) the Chief Executive Officer, Millennium Challenge Corporation; (29) the Deputy Assistant to the President and Director, Office of Administration Executive Office of the President; (30) the Associate Commissioner, Office of Security and Emergency Preparedness, Social Security Administration; and (31) the Chief Postal Inspector, United States Postal Service.

1-104. Security Cognizance

a. Consistent with paragraph 1-101e, security cognizance remains with each Federal department or agency unless lawfully delegated. The term Cognizant Security Agency (CSA) denotes the Department of Defense (DoD), the Department of Energy (DOE), the NRC, and the DNI. The Secretary of Defense, the Secretary of Energy, the DNI and the Chairman, NRC, may delegate any aspect of security administration regarding classified activities and contracts under their purview within the CSA or to another CSA. Responsibility for security administration may be further delegated by a CSA to one or more Cognizant Security Offices (CSO). It is the obligation of each CSA to inform industry of the applicable CSO.

b. The designation of a CSO does not relieve any Government Contracting Activity (GCA) of the responsibility to protect and safeguard the classified information necessary for its classified contracts, or from visiting the contractor to review the security aspects of such contracts.

c. Nothing in this Manual affects the authority of the Head of an Agency to limit, deny, or revoke access to classified information under its statutory, regulatory, or contract jurisdiction if that Agency Head determines that the security of the nation so requires. The term "Agency Head" has the meaning provided in Title 5 United States Code (U.S.C.) Section 552(f) (reference (h)).

1-105. Composition of Manual. This Manual is comprised of a "baseline" portion (Chapters 1 through 11). The portion of the Manual that prescribes requirements, restrictions, and safeguards that exceed the baseline standards, such as those necessary to protect special classes of information, is included in the NISPOM Supplement (NISPOMSUP). Until officially revised or canceled, the existing Carrier Supplement to the former "Industrial Security Manual for Safeguarding Classified Information" (reference (i)) will continue to be applicable to DoD-cleared facilities only.

1-106. Manual Interpretations. All contractor requests for interpretations of this Manual shall be forwarded to the CSA through its designated CSO. Requests for interpretation by contractors located on any U.S. Government installation shall be forwarded to the CSA through the commander or head of the host installation. Requests for interpretation of Director of Central Intelligence Directives (DCIDs) shall be forwarded to the DNI through approved channels.

1-107. Waivers and Exceptions to this Manual. Requests shall be submitted by industry through government channels approved by the CSA. When submitting a request for waiver, the contractor shall specify, in writing, the reasons why it is impractical or unreasonable to comply with the requirement. Waivers and exceptions will not be granted to impose more stringent protection requirements than this Manual provides for CONFIDENTIAL, SECRET, or TOP SECRET information.

1-108. Releasability and Effective Date

a. **Cleared for public release.** This manual is available on the Internet from the DoD Issuances Website at http://www.dtic.mil/whs/directives.

b. Is effective February 28, 2006.

Section 2. General Requirements

1-200. General. Contractors shall protect all classified information to which they have access or custody. A contractor performing work within the confines of a Federal installation shall safeguard classified information according to the procedures of the host installation or agency.

1-201. Facility Security Officer (FSO). The contractor shall appoint a U.S. citizen employee, who is cleared as part of the facility clearance (FCL) to be the FSO. The FSO will supervise and direct security measures necessary for implementing applicable requirements of this Manual and related Federal requirements for classified information. The FSO, or those otherwise performing security duties, shall complete security training as specified in Chapter 3 and as deemed appropriate by the CSA.

1-202. Insider Threat Program.

a. The contractor will establish and maintain an insider threat program that will gather, integrate, and report relevant and available information indicative of a potential or actual insider threat, consistent with E.O. 13587 (reference (ac)) and the National Insider Threat Policy and Minimum Standards for Executive Branch Insider Threat Programs (reference (ad)), as required by the appropriate CSA.

b. The contractor will designate a U.S. citizen employee, who is a senior official and cleared in connection with the FCL, to establish and execute an insider threat program. This Insider Threat Program Senior Official may also serve as the FSO. If the designated senior official is not also the FSO, the contractor's Insider Threat Program Senior Official will assure that the FSO is an integral member of the contractor's implementation program for an insider threat program.

c. A corporate family may choose to establish a corporate-wide insider threat program with one senior official designated to establish and execute the program. Each cleared legal entity using the corporate-wide Insider Threat Program Senior Official must separately designate that person as the Insider Threat Program Senior Official for that legal entity.

1-203. Standard Practice Procedures. The contractor shall implement all applicable terms of this Manual at each of its cleared facilities. Written procedures shall be prepared when the FSO believes them to be necessary for effective implementation of this Manual or when the CSA determines them to be necessary to reasonably exclude the possibility of loss or compromise of classified information.

1-204. One-Person Facilities. A facility at which only one person is assigned shall establish procedures for CSA notification after death or incapacitation of that person. The current combination of the facility's security container shall be provided to the CSA, or in the case of a multiple facility organization, to the home office.

1-205. Cooperation with Federal Agencies and Officially Credentialed Representatives of Those Agencies. Contractors shall cooperate with Federal agencies and their officially credentialed representatives during official inspections, investigations concerning the protection of classified information and during personnel security investigations of present or former employees and others. Cooperation includes providing suitable arrangements within the facility for conducting private interviews with employees during normal working hours, providing relevant employment and security records and records pertinent to insider threat (e.g., security, cybersecurity and human resources) for review when requested, and rendering other necessary assistance.

1-206. Security Training and Briefings. Contractors are responsible for advising all cleared employees, including those outside the United States, of their individual responsibility for safeguarding classified information. In this regard, contractors shall provide security training as appropriate, according to Chapter 3, to cleared employees by initial briefings, refresher briefings, and debriefings.

1-207. Security Reviews

a. **Government Reviews.** Aperiodic security reviews of all cleared contractor facilities will be conducted to ensure that safeguards employed by contractors are adequate for the protection of classified information.

(1) **Review Cycle.** The CSA will determine the frequency of security reviews, which may be increased or decreased consistent with risk management principles. Security reviews may be

conducted not more often than once every 12 months unless special circumstances exist.

(2) **Procedures.** Contractors will normally be provided notice of a forthcoming review. Unannounced reviews may be conducted at the discretion of the CSA. Security reviews necessarily subject all contractor employees and all areas and receptacles under the control of the contractor to examination. However, every effort will be made to avoid unnecessary intrusion into the personal effects of contractor personnel. The physical examination of the interior space of equipment not authorized to secure classified material will always be accomplished in the presence of a representative of the contractor.

(3) **Reciprocity.** Each CSA is responsible for ensuring that redundant and duplicative security review and audit activity of its contractors is held to a minimum, including such activity conducted at common facilities by other CSA's. Appropriate intra- and/or inter-agency agreements shall be executed to avoid redundant and duplicate reviews. Instances of redundant and duplicative security review and audit activity shall be reported to the Director, ISOO, for resolution.

b. **Contractor Reviews.** Contractors shall review their security system on a continuing basis and shall also conduct a formal self-inspection, including the self-inspection required by paragraph 8-101h of chapter 8 of this Manual, at intervals consistent with risk management principles.

(1) These self-inspections will be related to the activity, information, information systems (ISs), and conditions of the overall security program, to include the insider threat program; have sufficient scope, depth, and frequency; and management support in execution and remedy.

(2) The contractor will prepare a formal report describing the self-inspection, its findings, and resolution of issues found. The contractor will retain the formal report for CSA review through the next CSA inspection.

(3) A senior management official at the cleared facility will certify to the CSA, in writing on an annual basis, that a self-inspection has been conducted, that senior management has been briefed on the results, that appropriate corrective action has been taken, and that management fully supports the security program at the cleared facility.

(4) Self-inspections by contractors will include the review of representative samples of the contractor's derivative classification actions, as applicable.

1-208. Hotlines. Federal agencies maintain hotlines to provide an unconstrained avenue for government and contractor employees to report, without fear of reprisal, known or suspected instances of serious security irregularities and infractions concerning contracts, programs, or projects. These hotlines do not supplant contractor responsibility to facilitate reporting and timely investigation of security matters concerning its operations or personnel, and contractor personnel are encouraged to furnish information through established company channels. However, the hotline may be used as an alternate means to report this type of information when considered prudent or necessary. Contractors shall inform all employees that the hotlines may be used, if necessary, for reporting matters of national security significance. CSA hotline addresses and telephone numbers are as follows:

Defense Hotline
The Pentagon
Washington, DC 20301-1900
(800) 424-9098

U.S. Nuclear Regulatory Commission
Office of the Inspector General
Hotline Program, MS 05 E13
11555 Rockville Pike
Rockville, MD 20852-2738
1-800-233-3497
TDD: 1-800-270-2787

DOE Hotline
Department of Energy
Office of the Inspector General
1000 Independence Avenue, S.W. Room SD-031
Washington, D.C. 20585
(202) 586-4073
(800) 541-1625

DNI Hotline
Director of National Intelligence
Office of the Inspector General
Washington, D.C. 20511
(703) 482-2650

1-209. Classified Information Procedures Act (CIPA) (Public Law. 96-456, 94 Stat. 2025 codified at Title 18 U.S.C. Appendix 3 (reference (j))). The CIPA provides procedures for access to classified information by defendants and their representatives in criminal proceedings in U.S. District Courts, U.S. Courts of Appeal, and the U.S. Supreme Court. The provisions of this Manual do not apply to criminal proceedings in the courts and do not authorize contractors or their employees to release classified information in connection with any criminal proceedings.

Section 3. Reporting Requirements

1-300. General. Contractors are required to report certain events that: impact the status of the facility clearance (FCL); impact the status of an employee's personnel security clearance (PCL); may indicate the employee poses an insider threat; affect proper safeguarding of classified information, or that indicate classified information has been lost or compromised.

a. Contractors shall establish such internal procedures as are necessary to ensure that cleared employees are aware of their responsibilities for reporting pertinent information to the FSO, the Federal Bureau of Investigation (FBI), or other Federal authorities as required by this Manual, the terms of a classified contract, and U.S. law. Contractors shall provide complete information to enable the CSA to ascertain whether classified information is adequately protected. Contractors shall submit reports to the FBI and to their CSA as specified in this section.

b. When the reports are classified or offered in confidence and so marked by the contractor, the information will be reviewed by the CSA to determine whether it may be withheld from public disclosure under applicable exemptions of the Freedom of Information Act (5 U.S.C. 552) (reference (k)).

c. When the reports are unclassified and contain information pertaining to an individual, the Privacy Act of 1974 (5 U.S.C. 552a)(reference (l)) permits withholding of that information from the individual only to the extent that the disclosure of the information would reveal the identity of a source who furnished the information to the U.S. Government under an expressed promise that the identity of the source would be held in confidence. The fact that a report is submitted in confidence must be clearly marked on the report.

1-301. Reports to be Submitted to the FBI. The contractor shall promptly submit a written report to the nearest field office of the FBI regarding information coming to the contractor's attention concerning actual, probable or possible espionage, sabotage, terrorism, or subversive activities at any of its locations. An initial report may be made by phone, but it must be followed in writing, regardless of the disposition made of the report by the FBI. A copy of the written report shall be provided to the CSA.

1-302. Reports to be Submitted to the CSA

a. **Adverse Information.** Contractors shall report adverse information coming to their attention concerning any of their cleared employees. Reports based on rumor or innuendo should not be made. The subsequent termination of employment of an employee does not obviate the requirement to submit this report. If the individual is employed on a Federal installation, the contractor shall furnish a copy of the report and its final disposition to the commander or head of the installation.

NOTE: In Taglia vs. Philco (372 F.2d 771), the U.S. Court of Appeals for the 4th Circuit decided that a contractor is not liable for defamation of an employee because of reports made to the Government under the requirements of this Manual and its previous versions. In Becker v. Philco (389 U.S. 979), the U.S. Supreme Court denied the appeal from the 4th Circuit.

b. **Suspicious Contacts.** Contractors shall report efforts by any individual, regardless of nationality, to obtain illegal or unauthorized access to classified information or to compromise a cleared employee. In addition, all contacts by cleared employees with known or suspected intelligence officers from any country, or any contact which suggests the employee concerned may be the target of an attempted exploitation by the intelligence services of another country shall be reported.

c. **Change in Cleared Employee Status.** Contractors shall report: (1) the death; (2) a change in name; (3) the termination of employment; (4) change in citizenship; and (5) when the possibility of access to classified information in the future has been reasonably foreclosed. The CSA shall designate the appropriate reporting mechanism.

d. **Citizenship by Naturalization.** Contractors shall report if a non-U.S. citizen employee granted a Limited Access Authorization (LAA) becomes a citizen through naturalization. The report shall include: (1) city, county, and state where naturalized; (2) date naturalized; (3) court; and (4) certificate number.

e. **Employees Desiring Not to Perform on Classified Work.** Contractors shall report that an employee no longer wishes to be processed for a clearance or to continue an existing clearance.

f. Standard Form (SF) 312. Refusal by an employee to execute the "Classified Information Nondisclosure Agreement" (SF 312).

g. Change Conditions Affecting the Facility Clearance

(1) Any change of ownership, including stock transfers that affect control of the company.

(2) Any change of operating name or address of the company or any of its cleared locations.

(3) Any change to the information previously submitted for key management personnel including, as appropriate, the names of the individuals they are replacing. In addition, a statement shall be made indicating (a) whether the new key management personnel are cleared, and if so, to what level and when, their dates and places of birth, social security numbers, and their citizenship; (b) whether they have been excluded from access; or (c) whether they have been temporarily excluded from access pending the granting of their clearance. A new complete listing of key management personnel need be submitted only at the discretion of the contractor and/or when requested by the CSA.

(4) Action to terminate business or operations for any reason, imminent adjudication or reorganization in bankruptcy, or any change that might affect the validity of the FCL.

(5) Any material change concerning the information previously reported by the contractor concerning foreign ownership, control or influence (FOCI). This report shall be made by the submission of a Certificate Pertaining to Foreign Interests. When submitting this information, it is not necessary to repeat answers that have not changed. When entering into discussions, consultations or agreements that may reasonably lead to effective ownership or control by a foreign interest, the contractor shall report the details by letter. If the contractor has received a Schedule 13D from the investor, a copy shall be forwarded with the report.

h. Changes in Storage Capability. Any change in the storage capability that would raise or lower the level of classified information the facility is approved to safeguard.

i. Inability to Safeguard Classified Material. Any emergency situation that renders the facility incapable of safeguarding classified material.

j. Security Equipment Vulnerabilities. Significant vulnerabilities identified in security equipment, intrusion detection systems (IDS), access control systems, communications security (COMSEC) equipment or systems, and IS security hardware and software used to protect classified material.

k. Unauthorized Receipt of Classified Material. The receipt or discovery of any classified material that the contractor is not authorized to have. The report should identify the source of the material, originator, quantity, subject or title, date, and classification level.

l. Employee Information in Compromise Cases. When requested by the CSA, information concerning an employee when the information is needed in connection with the loss, compromise, or suspected compromise of classified information.

m. Disposition of Classified Material Terminated From Accountability. When the whereabouts or disposition of classified material previously terminated from accountability is subsequently determined.

n. Foreign Classified Contracts. Any precontract negotiation or award not placed through a GCA that involves, or may involve: (1) the release or disclosure of U.S. classified information to a foreign interest or (2) access to classified information furnished by a foreign interest.

1-303. Reports of Loss, Compromise, or Suspected Compromise. Any loss, compromise or suspected compromise of classified information, foreign or domestic, shall be reported to the CSA. Classified material that cannot be located within a reasonable period of time shall be presumed to be lost until an investigation determines otherwise. If the facility is located on a Government installation, the report shall be furnished to the CSA through the Commander or Head of the host installation.

a. Preliminary Inquiry. Immediately on receipt of a report of loss, compromise, or suspected compromise of classified information, the contractor shall initiate a preliminary inquiry to ascertain all of the circumstances surrounding the reported loss, compromise or suspected compromise.

b. Initial Report. If the contractor's preliminary inquiry confirms that a loss, compromise, or suspected compromise of any classified information occurred, the contractor shall promptly submit an initial report of the incident unless otherwise notified by the CSA. Submission of the initial report shall not be deferred.

c. Final Report. When the investigation has been completed, a final report shall be submitted to the CSA. The report should include:

(1) Material and relevant information that was not included in the initial report;

(2) The name and social security number of the individual(s) who was primarily responsible for the incident, including a record of prior loss, compromise, or suspected compromise for which the individual had been determined responsible;

(3) A statement of the corrective action taken to preclude a recurrence and the disciplinary action taken against the responsible individual(s), if any; and

(4) Specific reasons for reaching the conclusion that loss, compromise, or suspected compromise occurred or did not occur.

1-304. Individual Culpability Reports. Contractors shall establish and enforce policies that provide for appropriate administrative actions taken against employees who violate requirements of this Manual. They shall establish and apply a graduated scale of disciplinary actions in the event of employee violations or negligence. A statement of the administrative actions taken against an employee shall be included in a report to the CSA when individual responsibility for a security violation can be determined and one or more of the following factors are evident:

a. The violation involved a deliberate disregard of security requirements.

b. The violation involved gross negligence in the handling of classified material.

c. The violation involved was not deliberate in nature but involves a pattern of negligence or carelessness.

Section 4. Reports to DoD About Cyber Incidents On Cleared Defense Contractors (CDCs) IS Approved to Process Classified Information

1-400. General.

a. This section applies only to CDCs.

b. DoD will provide detailed reporting instructions via industrial security letter (ISL) in accordance with DoD Instruction 5220.22 (reference (ae)).

c. This section sets forth the CDC reporting requirements solely for any cyber incidents involving CDC covered ISs that have been approved by the designated DoD NISP CSO to process classified information, referred to in this Manual as a "classified covered IS." A classified covered IS will be considered a type of covered network consistent with the requirements of Section 941 of Public Law 112-239 (reference (af)), and section 391 of Title 10, U.S. code (reference (ag)). The reporting requirements of this section are in addition to the requirements in paragraphs 1-301 or 1-303 of section 3 of this Manual, which can include certain activities occurring on unclassified ISs.

1-401. Reports to be Submitted to DoD.

a. CDCs will report immediately to DoD any cyber incident on a classified covered IS, as described in paragraph 1-400c of this section.

b. At a minimum, CDCs will report:

(1) A description of the technique or method used in the cyber incident.

(2) A sample of the malicious software, if discovered and isolated by the CDC, involved in the cyber incident.

(3) A summary of information in connection with any DoD program that has been potentially compromised due to the cyber incident.

c. Information that is reported by the CDC (or derived from information reported by the CDC) will be safeguarded, used, and disseminated in a manner consistent with DoD procedures governing the handling of such information reported pursuant to references (af) and (ag) (e.g., as implemented at Part 236 of reference (z) and Subpart 204.73 of Title 48, CFR (reference (ah)), and subject to any additional restrictions based on the classification of the information.

1-402. Access to Equipment and Information by DoD Personnel.

a. DoD personnel, upon request to the CDC, may be required to obtain access to equipment or information of the CDC that is necessary to conduct forensic analysis in addition to any analysis conducted by the CDC.

b. When access to CDC classified ISs is required, the CDC is only required to provide DoD access to equipment or information, as described in paragraph 1-402a of this section to determine whether information was successfully exfiltrated from a CDC's classified covered IS and if so, what information was exfiltrated.

CHAPTER 2
Security Clearances

Section 1. Facility Clearances (FCLs)

2-100.   General.   An FCL is an administrative determination that a company is eligible for access to classified information or award of a classified contract.   Contract award may be made prior to the issuance of an FCL.   In those cases, the contractor will be processed for an FCL at the appropriate level and must meet eligibility requirements for access to classified information.   However, the contractor will not be afforded access to classified information until the FCL has been granted.   The FCL requirement for a prime contractor includes those instances in which all classified access will be limited to subcontractors. Contractors are eligible for custody (possession) of classified material if they have an FCL and storage capability approved by the CSA.

a.   An FCL is valid for access to classified information at the same or lower classification level as the FCL granted.

b.   FCLs will be registered centrally by the U.S. Government.

c.   A contractor shall not use its FCL for advertising or promotional purposes.

2-101.   Reciprocity.   An FCL shall be considered valid and acceptable for use on a fully reciprocal basis by all Federal departments and agencies, provided it meets or exceeds the level of clearance needed.

2-102.   Eligibility Requirements.   A contractor or prospective contractor cannot apply for its own FCL. A GCA or a currently cleared contractor may sponsor an uncleared company for an FCL.   A company must meet the following eligibility requirements before it can be processed for an FCL:

a.   The company must need access to the classified information in connection with a legitimate U.S. Government or foreign government requirement.

b.   The company must be organized and existing under the laws of any of the fifty states, the District of Columbia, or Puerto Rico, and be located in the United States or its territorial areas.

c.   The company must have a reputation for integrity and lawful conduct in its business dealings. The company and its key managers must not be barred from participating in U.S. Government contracts.

d.   The company must not be under FOCI to such a degree that the granting of the FCL would be inconsistent with the national interest.

2-103.   Processing the FCL.   The CSA will advise and assist the company during the FCL process. As a minimum, the company will:

a.   Execute CSA-designated forms.

b.   Process key management personnel for PCLs.

c.   Appoint a U.S. citizen employee as the FSO.

2-104.   PCLs Required in Connection with the FCL.   The senior management official, the FSO and the Insider Threat Program Senior Official must always be cleared to the level of the FCL.   Other officials, as determined by the CSA, must be granted PCLs or be excluded from classified access pursuant to paragraph 2-106.

2-105.   PCLs Concurrent with the FCL. Contractors may designate employees who require access to classified information during the negotiation of a contract or the preparation of a bid or quotation pertaining to a prime contract or a subcontract to be processed for PCLs concurrent with the FCL.   The granting of an FCL is not dependent on the clearance of such employees.

2-106.   Exclusion Procedures.   When, pursuant to paragraph 2-104, formal exclusion action is required, the organization's board of directors or similar executive body shall affirm the following, as appropriate.

a.   Such officers, directors, partners, regents, or trustees (designated by name) shall not require, shall not have, and can be effectively excluded from access to all classified information disclosed to the organization.   They also do not occupy positions that would enable them to adversely affect the organization's policies or practices in the performance of classified contracts. This action shall be made a matter of record by the organization's executive body. A copy of the resolution shall be furnished to the CSA.

b. Such officers or partners (designated by name) shall not require, shall not have, and can be effectively denied access to higher-level classified information (specify which higher level(s)) and do not occupy positions that would enable them to adversely affect the organization's policies or practices in the performance of higher-level classified contracts (specify higher level(s)). This action shall be made a matter of record by the organization's executive body. A copy of the resolution shall be furnished to the CSA.

2-107. Interim FCLs. An interim FCL may be granted to eligible contractors by the CSA. An interim FCL is granted on a temporary basis pending completion of the full investigative requirements.

2-108. Multiple Facility Organizations (MFOs). The home office facility must have an FCL at the same, or higher, level of any cleared facility within the MFO. The CSA shall determine the necessity for branch offices to be cleared.

2-109. Parent-Subsidiary Relationships. When a parent-subsidiary relationship exists, the parent and the subsidiary will be processed separately for an FCL. As a general rule, the parent must have an FCL at the same, or higher, level as the subsidiary. However, the CSA will determine the necessity for the parent to be cleared or excluded from access to classified information. The CSA will advise the companies as to what action is necessary for processing the FCL. When a parent or its cleared subsidiaries are collocated, a formal written agreement to use common security services may be executed by the two firms, subject to the approval of the CSA.

2-110. Termination of the FCL. Once granted, an FCL remains in effect until terminated by either party. If the FCL is terminated for any reason, the contractor shall return all classified material in its possession to the appropriate GCA or dispose of the material as instructed by the CSA.

2-111. Records Maintenance. Contractors shall maintain the original CSA designated forms for the duration of the FCL.

Section 2. Personnel Security Clearances

2-200. General

a. An employee may be processed for a PCL when the contractor determines that access is essential in the performance of tasks or services related to the fulfillment of a classified contract. A PCL is valid for access to classified information at the same or lower level of classification as the level of the clearance granted.

b. The CSA will determine eligibility for access to classified information in accordance with the national standards and notify the contractor that eligibility has been granted. The CSA will notify the contractor when an employee's PCL has been denied, suspended, or revoked. The contractor shall immediately deny access to classified information to any employee when notified of a denial, revocation or suspension. When the CSA has designated a database as the system of record for contractor eligibility and access, the contractor shall be responsible for annotating and maintaining the accuracy of their employees' access records. Specific procedures will be provided by the CSA.

c. Within an MFO or within the same corporate family, contractors may centrally manage eligibility and access records.

d. The contractor shall limit requests for PCLs to the minimal number of employees necessary for operational efficiency, consistent with contractual obligations and other requirements of this Manual. Requests for PCLs shall not be made to establish "pools" of cleared employees.

e. The contractor shall not submit a request for a PCL to one agency if the employee applicant is cleared or is in process for a PCL by another agency. In such cases, to permit clearance verification, the contractor should provide the new agency with the full name, date and place of birth, social security number, clearing agency and type of investigation

f. Access to SCI and SAP information is a determination made by the granting authority.

2-201. Investigative Requirements. Investigations conducted by a Federal agency shall not be duplicated by another Federal agency when those investigations are current within 5 years and meet the scope and standards for the level of PCL required. The types of investigations required are as follows:

a. **Single Scope Background Investigation (SSBI).** An SSBI is required for TOP SECRET, Q, and SCI access. Investigative requests shall be made using the electronic version of the Questionnaire for National Security Positions (SF 86).

b. **National Agency Check with Local Agency Check and Credit Check (NACLC).** An NACLC is required for a SECRET, L, and CONFIDENTIAL PCLs. Investigative requests shall be made using the electronic version of the SF 86.

c. **Polygraph.** Agencies with policies sanctioning the use of the polygraph for PCL purposes may require polygraph examinations when necessary. If issues of concern surface during any phase of security processing, coverage will be expanded to resolve those issues.

d. **Reinvestigation.** Contractor personnel may be subject to a reinvestigation program as specified by the CSA.

e. **Financial Disclosure**. When advised by the GCA that an employee is required to complete a Financial Disclosure Form, the contractor shall ensure that the employee has the opportunity to complete and submit the form in private.

2-202. Procedures for Completing the Electronic Version of the SF 86. The electronic version of the SF 86 shall be completed jointly by the employee and the FSO or an equivalent contractor employee(s) who has (have) been specifically designated by the contractor to review an employee's SF 86.

a. The FSO or designee shall inform the employee that the SF 86 is subject to review and shall review the application solely to determine its adequacy and to ensure that necessary information has not been omitted. The FSO or designee shall provide the employee with written notification that review of the information is for adequacy and completeness, information will be used for no other purpose within the company, and that the information provided by the employee is protected by reference (l). The FSO or designee shall not share information from the employee's SF 86 within the company and shall not use the information for any purpose other than determining the adequacy and completeness of the SF 86.

b. The FSO or designee shall ensure that the applicant's fingerprints are authentic, legible, and complete to avoid subsequent clearance processing delays. The FSO or designee shall retain an original, signed copy of the SF 86, the Authorization for Release of Information and Records, and Authorization for Release of Medical Information until the clearance process has been completed. The FSO or designee shall maintain the retained documentation in such a manner that the confidentiality of the documents is preserved and protected against access by anyone within the company other than the FSO or designee. When the applicant's eligibility for access to classified information has been granted or denied, the retained documentation shall be destroyed.

2-203. Common Adjudicative Standards. Security clearance and SCI access determinations are based upon uniform common adjudicative standards.

2-204. Reciprocity. Federal agencies that grant access to classified information to their employees or their contractor employees are responsible for determining whether such employees have been previously cleared or investigated by the Federal Government. Any previously granted PCL that is based upon a current investigation of a scope that meets or exceeds that necessary for the clearance required shall provide the basis for issuance of a new clearance without further investigation or adjudication unless significant derogatory information that was not previously adjudicated becomes known to the granting agency.

2-205. Pre-employment Clearance Action. If access to classified information is required by a potential employee immediately upon commencement of their employment, a PCL application may be submitted to the CSA by the contractor prior to the date of employment provided a written commitment for employment has been made by the contractor, and the candidate has accepted the offer in writing. The commitment for employment will indicate that employment shall commence within 30 days of the granting of eligibility for a PCL.

2-206. Contractor-Granted Clearances. Contractors are no longer permitted to grant clearances. Contractor-granted CONFIDENTIAL clearances in effect under previous policy are not valid for access to RD, FRD, COMSEC information, SCI, NATO information (except RESTRICTED), and classified foreign government information (FGI), or for Critical or Controlled Nuclear Weapon Security positions.

2-207. Verification of U.S. Citizenship. The contractor shall require each applicant for a PCL who claims U.S. citizenship to produce evidence of citizenship.

2-208. Acceptable Proof of Citizenship

a. For individuals born in the United States, a birth certificate is the primary and preferred means of citizenship verification. Acceptable certificates must show that the birth record was filed shortly after birth and it must be certified with the registrar's signature. It must bear the raised, impressed, or multicolored seal of the registrar's office. The only exception is if a State or other jurisdiction does not issue such seals as a matter of policy. Uncertified copies of birth certificates are not acceptable. A delayed birth certificate is one created when a record was filed more than one year after the date of birth. Such a certificate is acceptable if it shows that the report of birth was supported by acceptable secondary evidence of birth. Secondary evidence may include: baptismal or circumcision certificates, hospital birth records, or affidavits of persons having personal knowledge about the facts of birth. Other documentary evidence can be early census, school, or family bible records, newspaper files, or insurance papers. All documents submitted as evidence of birth in the U.S. shall be original or certified documents.

b. If the individual claims citizenship by naturalization, a certificate of naturalization is acceptable proof of citizenship.

c. If citizenship was acquired by birth abroad to a U.S. citizen parent or parents, the following are acceptable evidence:

(1) A Certificate of Citizenship issued by the Department of Homeland Security, U.S. Citizenship and Immigration Services (USCIS) or its predecessor organization.

(2) A Report of Birth Abroad of a Citizen of the United States of America

(3) A Certificate of Birth.

d. A passport, current or expired, is acceptable proof of citizenship.

e. A Record of Military Processing-Armed Forces of the United States (DD Form 1966) is acceptable proof of citizenship, provided it reflects U.S. citizenship.

2-209. Non-U.S. Citizens. Only U.S. citizens are eligible for a security clearance. Every effort shall be made to ensure that non-U.S. citizens are not employed in duties that may require access to classified information. However, compelling reasons may exist to grant access to classified information to a non-U.S. citizen. Such individuals may be granted a Limited Access Authorization (LAA) in those rare circumstances where the non-U.S. citizen possesses unique or unusual skill or expertise that is urgently needed to support a specific U.S. Government contract involving access to specified classified information and a cleared or clearable U.S. citizen is not readily available. In addition, the LAA may be processed only with the concurrence of the GCA.

2-210. Access Limitations of an LAA. An LAA granted under the provisions of this Manual is not valid for access to the following types of information:

a. TOP SECRET information.

b. RD or FRD.

c. Information that has not been determined releasable by a U.S. Government designated disclosure authority to the country of which the individual is a citizen.

d. COMSEC information.

e. Intelligence information.

f. NATO Information. However, foreign nationals of a NATO member nation may be authorized access to NATO Information provided that: (1) A NATO Security Clearance Certificate is obtained by the CSA from the individual's home country; and (2) NATO access is limited to performance on a specific NATO contract.

g. Information for which foreign disclosure has been prohibited in whole or in part; and

h. Information provided to the U.S. Government in confidence by a third party government and classified information furnished by a third party government.

2-211. Interim PCLs. Applicants for TOP SECRET, SECRET, and CONFIDENTIAL PCLs may be routinely granted interim PCLs, as appropriate, provided there is no evidence of adverse information of material significance. The interim status will cease if results are favorable following completion of full investigative requirements. Non-U.S. citizens are not eligible for access to classified information on an interim basis.

a. An interim SECRET or CONFIDENTIAL PCL is valid for access to classified information at the level of the eligibility granted, except for RD, COMSEC Information, and NATO information. An interim TOP SECRET PCL is valid for access to TOP SECRET information, RD, NATO Information, and COMSEC information at the SECRET and CONFIDENTIAL level. Access to SCI and SAP information based on an interim PCL is a determination made by the granting authority.

b. An interim PCL granted by the CSA negates any existing contractor-granted CONFIDENTIAL clearance. When an interim PCL has been granted and derogatory information is subsequently developed, the CSA may withdraw the interim pending completion of the processing that is a prerequisite to the granting of a final PCL.

c. When an interim PCL for an individual who is required to be cleared in connection with the FCL is withdrawn, the individual must be removed from access or the interim FCL will also be withdrawn.

d. Withdrawal of an interim PCL is not a denial or revocation of the clearance and may not be appealed.

2-212. Consultants. A consultant is an individual under contract to provide professional or technical assistance to a contractor in a capacity requiring access to classified information. The consultant shall not possess classified material off the premises of the using (hiring) contractor except in connection with authorized visits. The consultant and the using contractor shall jointly execute a consultant certificate setting forth respective security responsibilities. The using contractor shall be the consumer of the services offered by the consultant it sponsors for a PCL. For security administration purposes, the consultant shall be considered an employee of the using contractor. Consultants to GCAs shall be processed for PCLs by the GCA in accordance with GCA procedures.

Section 3. Foreign Ownership, Control, or Influence (FOCI)

2-300. Policy. Foreign investment can play an important role in maintaining the vitality of the U.S. industrial base. Therefore, it is the policy of the U.S. Government to allow foreign investment consistent with the national security interests of the United States. The following FOCI policy for U.S. companies subject to an FCL is intended to facilitate foreign investment by ensuring that foreign firms cannot undermine U.S. security and export controls to gain unauthorized access to critical technology, classified information, and special classes of classified information.

a. A U.S. company is considered under FOCI whenever a foreign interest has the power, direct or indirect, whether or not exercised, and whether or not exercisable through the ownership of the U.S. company's securities, by contractual arrangements or other means, to direct or decide matters affecting the management or operations of that company in a manner which may result in unauthorized access to classified information or may adversely affect the performance of classified contracts.

b. Whenever a company has been determined to be under FOCI, the primary consideration shall be the safeguarding of classified information. The CSA is responsible for taking whatever interim action is necessary to safeguard classified information, in coordination with other affected agencies as appropriate.

c. A U.S. company determined to be under FOCI is ineligible for an FCL unless and until security measures have been put in place to negate or mitigate FOCI. When a contractor determined to be under FOCI is negotiating an acceptable FOCI mitigation/negation measure, an existing FCL shall continue so long as there is no indication that classified information is at risk of compromise. An existing FCL shall be invalidated if the contractor is unable or unwilling to negotiate an acceptable FOCI mitigation/negation measure. An existing FCL shall be revoked if security measures cannot be taken to remove the possibility of unauthorized access or adverse affect on classified contracts.

d. If the company does not have possession of classified material, and does not have a current or impending requirement for access to classified information, the FCL shall be administratively terminated.

e. Changed conditions, such as a change in ownership, indebtedness, or the foreign intelligence threat, may justify certain adjustments to the security terms under which a company is operating or, alternatively, that a different FOCI negation method be employed. If a changed condition is of sufficient significance, it might also result in a determination that a company is no longer considered to be under FOCI or, conversely, that a company is no longer eligible for an FCL.

f. The Federal Government reserves the right and has the obligation to impose any security method, safeguard, or restriction it believes necessary to ensure that unauthorized access to classified information is effectively precluded and that performance of classified contracts is not adversely affected.

g. Nothing contained in this section shall affect the authority of the Head of an Agency to limit, deny or revoke access to classified information under its statutory, regulatory or contract jurisdiction. For purposes of this section, the term "Agency" has the meaning provided at reference (h), to include the term "DoD Component."

2-301. Factors. The following factors relating to the company, the foreign interest, and the government of the foreign interest, as appropriate, shall be considered in the aggregate to determine whether an applicant company is under FOCI, its eligibility for an FCL, and the protective measures required:

a. Record of economic and government espionage against U.S. targets.

b. Record of enforcement and/or engagement in unauthorized technology transfer.

c. The type and sensitivity of the information that shall be accessed.

d. The source, nature and extent of FOCI, including whether foreign interests hold a majority or substantial minority position in the company, taking into consideration the immediate, intermediate, and ultimate parent companies. A minority position is deemed substantial if it consists of greater than 5 percent of the ownership interests or greater than 10 percent of the voting interest.

e. Record of compliance with pertinent U.S. laws, regulations and contracts.

f. The nature of any bilateral and multilateral security and information exchange agreements that may pertain.

g. Ownership or control, in whole or in part, by a foreign government.

2-302. Procedures. A company is required to complete a Certificate Pertaining to Foreign Interests when applying for an FCL or when significant changes occur to information previously submitted. In the case of a corporate family, the form shall be a consolidated response rather than separate submissions from individual members of the corporate family.

a. If there are any affirmative answers on the Certificate Pertaining to Foreign Interests, or other information is received which indicates that the applicant company may be under FOCI, the CSA shall review the case to determine the relative significance of the information in regard to:

(1) Whether the applicant is under FOCI,

(2) The extent and manner to which the FOCI may result in unauthorized access to classified information or adversely impact classified contract performance; and

(3) The type of actions, if any, that would be necessary to negate the effects of FOCI to a level deemed acceptable to the Federal Government. Disputed matters may be appealed and the applicant shall be advised of the government's appeal channels by the CSA.

b. When a contractor with an FCL enters into negotiations for the proposed merger, acquisition, or takeover by a foreign interest, the contractor shall submit notification to the CSA of the commencement of such negotiations. The submission shall include the type of transaction under negotiation (stock purchase, asset purchase, etc.), the identity of the potential foreign interest investor, and a plan to negate the FOCI by a method outlined in 2-303. The company shall submit copies of loan, purchase and shareholder agreements, annual reports, bylaws, articles of incorporation, partnership agreements, and reports filed with other Federal agencies to the CSA.

c. When factors not related to ownership are present, positive measures shall assure that the foreign interest can be effectively mitigated and cannot otherwise adversely affect performance on classified contracts. Examples of such measures include modification or termination of loan agreements, contracts and other understandings with foreign interests; diversification or reduction of foreign-source income; demonstration of financial viability independent of foreign interests; elimination or resolution of problem debt; assignment of specific oversight duties and responsibilities to board members; formulation of special executive-level security committees to consider and oversee matters that affect the performance of classified contracts; physical or organizational separation of the contractor component performing on classified contracts; the appointment of a technology control officer; adoption of special Board Resolutions; and other actions that negate or mitigate foreign influence.

2-303. FOCI Action Plans. The following are the methods that can be applied to negate or mitigate the risk of foreign ownership or control.

a. **Board Resolution.** When a foreign interest does not own voting interests sufficient to elect, or otherwise is not entitled to representation on the company's governing board, a resolution(s) by the governing board shall normally be adequate. The governing board shall identify the foreign shareholder and describe the type and number of foreign-owned shares; acknowledge the company's obligation to comply with all industrial security program and export control requirements; and certify that the foreign owner does not require, shall not have, and can be effectively precluded from unauthorized access to all classified and export-controlled information entrusted to or held by the company. The governing board shall provide for annual certifications to the CSA acknowledging the continued effectiveness of the resolution. The company shall distribute to members of its governing board and to its key management personnel copies of such resolutions, and report in the company's corporate records the completion of such distribution.

b. **Voting Trust Agreement and Proxy Agreement.** The Voting Trust Agreement and the Proxy Agreement are arrangements whereby the foreign owner relinquishes most rights associated with ownership of the company to cleared U.S. citizens approved by the U.S. Government. Under a Voting Trust Agreement, the foreign owner transfers legal title in the company to the Trustees. Under a Proxy Agreement, the foreign owner's voting rights are conveyed to the Proxy Holders. Neither arrangement imposes any restrictions on the company's eligibility to have access to classified information or to compete for classified contracts.

(1) Establishment of a Voting Trust or Proxy Agreement involves the selection of Trustees or Proxy Holders, all of whom must become members of the company's governing board. Both arrangements must provide for the exercise of all prerogatives of ownership by the Trustees or Proxy Holders with complete freedom to act independently from the foreign owners, except as provided in the Voting Trust or Proxy Agreement. The arrangements may, however, limit the authority of the Trustees or Proxy Holders by requiring that approval be obtained from the foreign owner(s) with respect to matters such as:

(a) The sale or disposal of the company's assets or a substantial part thereof;

(b) Pledges, mortgages, or other encumbrances on the company's assets, capital stock or ownership interests;

(c) Mergers, consolidations, or reorganizations;

(d) Dissolution; and

(e) Filing of a bankruptcy petition.

However, the Trustees or Proxy Holders may consult with the foreign owner, or vice versa, where otherwise consistent with U.S. laws, regulations and the terms of the Voting Trust or Proxy Agreement.

(2) The Trustees or Proxy Holders assume full responsibility for the foreign owner's voting interests and for exercising all management prerogatives relating thereto in such a way as to ensure that the foreign owner shall be insulated from the company, thereby solely retaining the status of a beneficiary. The company must be organized, structured, and financed so as to be capable of operating as a viable business entity independent from the foreign owner.

c. **Special Security Agreement (SSA) and Security Control Agreement (SCA).** The SSA and SCA are arrangements that, based upon an assessment of the FOCI factors, impose various industrial security and export control measures within an institutionalized set of company practices and procedures. They require active involvement in security matters of senior management and certain Board members (outside directors), who must be cleared U.S. citizens; provide for the establishment of a Government Security Committee (GSC) to oversee classified and export control matters; and preserve the foreign owner's right to be represented on the Board (inside directors) with a direct voice in the business management of the company while denying unauthorized access to classified information.

(1) When a company is not effectively owned or controlled by a foreign interest and the foreign interest is nevertheless entitled to representation on the company's governing board, the company may be cleared under an SCA. There are no access limitations under an SCA.

(2) A company that is effectively owned or controlled by a foreign interest may be cleared under an SSA arrangement. Access to proscribed information[6] by a company cleared under an SSA may require that the GCA complete a National Interest Determination (NID) to determine that release of proscribed information to the company is consistent with the national security interests of the United States, in accordance with part 2004 of reference (z). The CSA shall advise the GCA on the need for a NID.

(a) The NID can be program, project or contract specific. A separate NID is not required for each contract under a program or project. The NID decision shall be made at the GCA's Program Executive Office level. If the proscribed information is under the classification or control jurisdiction of another agency, the GCA shall advise that agency; e.g., National Security Agency (NSA) for COMSEC, DNI for SCI, DOE for RD. These agencies may determine that release to the contractor of an entire category of information under their control may not harm the national security.

(b) The GCA shall forward the completed NID to the CSA. The CSA shall not delay implementation of a FOCI action plan pending completion of a GCA's NID process as long as there is no indication that a NID shall be denied.

2-304. Citizenship of Persons Requiring PCLs. Under all methods of FOCI mitigation or negation,

---

[6] Proscribed information includes TS, COMSEC information or material, excluding controlled cryptographic items when unkeyed or utilized with unclassified keys; RD as defined in reference (c), SAP information; or SCI.

management positions requiring PCLs in conjunction with the FCL must be filled by U.S. citizens residing in the United States.

2-305. Qualifications of Trustees, Proxy Holders, and Outside Directors. Individuals who serve as Trustees, Proxy Holders, or Outside Directors must be:

a. Resident U.S. citizens who can exercise management prerogatives relating to their position in a way that ensures that the foreign owner can be effectively insulated from the company;

b. Except as approved by the CSA in advance and in writing, completely disinterested individuals with no prior involvement with the company, the entities with which it is affiliated, or the foreign owner; and

c. Issued a PCL at the level of the facility's FCL.

2-306. GSC. Under a Voting Trust, Proxy Agreement, SSA and SCA, the contractor is required to establish a permanent committee of its Board of Directors, known as the GSC.

a. Unless otherwise approved by the CSA, the GSC consists of Voting Trustees, Proxy Holders or Outside Directors, as applicable, and those officers/directors who hold PCLs.

b. The members of the GSC are required to ensure that the contractor maintains policies and procedures to safeguard classified and export controlled information entrusted to it, and that violations of those policies and procedures are promptly investigated and reported to the appropriate authority when it has been determined that a violation has occurred.

c. The GSC shall also take the necessary steps to ensure that the contractor complies with U.S. export control laws and regulations and does not take action deemed adverse to performance on classified contracts. This shall include the appointment of a Technology Control Officer (TCO) and the establishment of Technology Control Plan (TCP).

d. The contractor's FSO shall be the principal advisor to the GSC and attend GSC meetings. The Chairman of the GSC must concur with the appointment and replacement of FSOs selected by

management. The FSO and TCO functions shall be carried out under the authority of the GSC.

2-307. TCP. A TCP approved by the CSA shall be developed and implemented by those companies cleared under a Voting Trust Agreement, Proxy Agreement, SSA and SCA and when otherwise deemed appropriate by the CSA. The TCP shall prescribe all security measures determined necessary to reasonably foreclose the possibility of inadvertent access by non-U.S. citizen employees and visitors to information for which they are not authorized. The TCP shall also prescribe measures designed to assure that access by non-U.S. citizens is strictly limited to only that specific information for which appropriate Federal Government disclosure authorization has been obtained; e.g., an approved export license or technical assistance agreement. Unique badging, escort, segregated work area, security indoctrination schemes, and other measures shall be included, as appropriate.

2-308. Annual Review and Certification

a. **Annual Review.** The CSA shall meet at least annually with the GSCs of contractors operating under a Voting Trust, Proxy Agreement, SSA, or SCA to review the purpose and effectiveness of the clearance arrangement and to establish common understanding of the operating requirements and their implementation. These reviews shall also include an examination of the following:

(1) Acts of compliance or noncompliance with the approved security arrangement, standard rules, and applicable laws and regulations;

(2) Problems or impediments associated with the practical application or utility of the security arrangement; and

(3) Whether security controls, practices, or procedures warrant adjustment.

b. **Annual Certification.** For contractors operating under a Voting Trust Agreement, Proxy Agreement, SSA or SCA, the Chairman of the GSC shall submit to the CSA one year from the effective date of the agreement and annually thereafter an implementation and compliance report. Such reports shall include the following:

(1) A detailed description of the manner in which the contractor is carrying out its obligations under the agreement;

(2) Changes to security procedures, implemented or proposed, and the reasons for those changes;

(3) A detailed description of any acts of noncompliance, whether inadvertent or intentional, with a discussion of steps that were taken to prevent such acts from recurring;

(4) Any changes, or impending changes, of key management personnel or key board members, including the reasons therefore;

(5) Any changes or impending changes in the organizational structure or ownership, including any acquisitions, mergers or divestitures; and

(6) Any other issues that could have a bearing on the effectiveness of the applicable agreement.

2-309. Limited FCL. The United States has entered into Industrial Security Agreements with certain foreign governments. Some of these agreements establish arrangements whereby a foreign-owned U.S. company may be considered eligible for an FCL without any additional FOCI negation or mitigation instrument. Access limitations are inherent with the granting of Limited FCLs and are imposed upon all of the company's employees regardless of citizenship.

a. A Limited FCL may be granted upon satisfaction of the following criteria:

(1) There is an Industrial Security Agreement with the foreign government of the country from which the foreign ownership is derived.

(2) Release of classified information is in conformity with the U.S. National Disclosure Policy. Key management personnel may be citizens of the country of ownership for whom the United States has obtained security assurances at the appropriate level.

b. In extraordinary circumstances, a Limited FCL may also be granted even if the above criteria cannot be satisfied if there is a compelling need to do so consistent with U.S. national security interests. In

any such case, the GCA shall provide a compelling need statement to the CSA to justify the FCL and verify that access to classified information is essential for contract performance. The CSA shall acknowledge the existence of a Limited FCL only to that GCA.

2-310. Foreign Mergers, Acquisitions and Takeovers, and the Committee on Foreign Investment in the United States (CFIUS)

a. The CFIUS, an interagency committee chaired by the Treasury Department, conducts reviews of proposed mergers, acquisition or takeovers of U.S. persons by foreign interests under section 721 (Exon-Florio amendment) of the Defense Production Act (reference (m)). CFIUS review is a voluntary process and affords an opportunity to foreign persons and U.S. persons entering into a covered transaction to submit the transaction for review by CFIUS to assess the impact of the transaction on U.S. national security.

b. The CFIUS review and the CSA industrial security FOCI review are carried out in two parallel but separate processes with different time constraints and considerations.

c. If a transaction under CFIUS review would require FOCI negation or mitigation measures if consummated, the CSA shall promptly advise the parties to the transaction and request that they submit to the CSA a plan to negate or mitigate FOCI. If it appears that an agreement cannot be reached on material terms of a FOCI action plan, or if the U.S. party to the proposed transaction fails to comply with the FOCI reporting requirements of this Manual, the CSA may recommend a full investigation of the transaction by CFIUS to determine the effects on national security.

d. If the CSA becomes aware of a proposed transaction that should be reviewed by CFIUS, and the parties thereto do not file a joint voluntary notice with CFIUS to initiate review within a reasonable time, the CSA shall initiate action to have CFIUS notified.

CHAPTER 3
Security Training and Briefings

Section 1. Security Training and Briefings

3-100. General. Contractors shall provide all cleared employees with security training and briefings commensurate with their involvement with classified information.

3-101. Training Materials. Contractors may obtain defensive security, threat awareness, and other education and training information and material from their CSA or other sources.

3-102. FSO Training. Contractors shall be responsible for ensuring that the FSO, and others performing security duties, complete training considered appropriate by the CSA. Training requirements shall be based on the facility's involvement with classified information and may include an FSO orientation course and for FSOs at facilities with safeguarding capability, an FSO Program Management Course. Training, if required, should be completed within 1 year of appointment to the position of FSO.

3-103. Insider Threat Training. The designated Insider Threat Program Senior Official will ensure that contractor program personnel assigned insider threat program responsibilities and all other cleared employees complete training that the CSA considers appropriate.

a. Contractor insider threat program personnel, including the contractor designated Insider Threat Program Senior Official, must be trained in:

(1) Counterintelligence and security fundamentals, including applicable legal issues.

(2) Procedures for conducting insider threat response actions.

(3) Applicable laws and regulations regarding the gathering, integration, retention, safeguarding, and use of records and data, including the consequences of misuse of such information.

(4) Applicable legal, civil liberties, and privacy policies.

b. All cleared employees must be provided insider threat awareness training before being granted access to classified information, and annually thereafter. Training will address current and potential threats in the work and personal environment and will include at a minimum:

(1) The importance of detecting potential insider threats by cleared employees and reporting suspected activity to the insider threat program designee.

(2) Methodologies of adversaries to recruit trusted insiders and collect classified information, in particular within ISs.

(3) Indicators of insider threat behavior, and procedures to report such behavior.

(4) Counterintelligence and security reporting requirements, as applicable.

c. The contractor will establish and maintain a record of all cleared employees who have completed the initial and annual insider threat training. Depending on CSA-specific guidance, a CSA may, instead, conduct such training and retain the records.

3-104. Government-Provided Briefings. The CSA is responsible for providing initial security briefings to the FSO and for ensuring that other briefings required for special categories of information are provided.

3-105. Temporary Help Suppliers. A temporary help supplier, or other contractor who employs cleared individuals solely for dispatch elsewhere, shall be responsible for ensuring that required briefings are provided to their cleared personnel. The temporary help supplier or the using contractor may conduct these briefings.

3-106. Classified Information Nondisclosure Agreement (SF 312). The SF 312 is an agreement between the United States and an individual who is cleared for access to classified information. An employee issued an initial PCL must execute an SF 312 prior to being granted access to classified information. The contractor shall forward the executed SF 312 to the CSA for retention. If the employee refuses to execute the SF 312, the contractor shall deny the employee access to classified information and submit a report to the CSA. The SF 312 shall be signed and dated by the employee and witnessed. The employee's and witness' signatures must bear the same date.

3-107. Initial Security Briefings. Prior to being granted access to classified information, an employee shall receive an initial security briefing that includes the following:

a. A threat awareness security briefing, including insider threat awareness in accordance with paragraph 3-103b of this Manual.

b. A counterintelligence awareness briefing.

c. An overview of the security classification system.

d. Employee reporting obligations and requirements, including insider threat.

e. Initial and annual refresher cybersecurity awareness training for all authorized IS users (see chapter 8, paragraph 8-101c, of this Manual).

f. Security procedures and duties applicable to the employee's job.

3-108. Refresher Training. The contractor shall provide all cleared employees with some form of security education and training at least annually. Refresher training shall reinforce the information provided during the initial security briefing and shall keep cleared employees informed of appropriate changes in security regulations. See paragraph 8-103c of chapter 8 of this Manual for the requirement for IS security refresher training. Training methods may include group briefings, interactive videos, dissemination of instructional materials, or other media and methods. Contractors shall maintain records about the programs offered and employee participation in them. This requirement may be satisfied by use of distribution lists, facility/department-wide newsletters, or other means acceptable to the FSO.

3-109. Debriefings. Contractors shall debrief cleared employees at the time of termination of employment (discharge, resignation, or retirement); when an employee's PCL is terminated, suspended, or revoked; and upon termination of the FCL.

CHAPTER 4
Classification and Marking

Section 1. Classification

4-100. General. Information is classified under reference (b) by an original classification authority and is designated and marked as TOP SECRET, SECRET, or CONFIDENTIAL. The designation UNCLASSIFIED is used to identify information that does not require a security classification. Except as provided by statute, no other terms may be used to identify classified information.

4-101. Original Classification. An original classification decision at any level can be made only by a U.S. Government official who has been designated or delegated the authority in writing. A determination to originally classify information may be made only when (a) an original classification authority is classifying the information; (b) the information falls into one or more of the categories set forth in reference (b); (c) the unauthorized disclosure of the information, either by itself or in context with other information, reasonably could be expected to cause damage to the national security, which includes defense against transnational terrorism, that can be identified or described by the original classifier; and (d) the information is owned by, produced by or for, or is under the control of the U. S. Government. The original classifier must state the concise "Reason" for classification on the front of the document. The original classifier must also indicate either a date or event for the duration of classification for up to 10 years from the date of the original classification decision unless the date is further extended due to information sensitivities for up to 25 years. An original classification authority's agency must obtain the approval of the Interagency Security Classification Appeals Panel in order to continue the classification of information beyond 25 years.

4-102. Derivative Classification Responsibilities

a. Contractor personnel make derivative classification decisions when they incorporate, paraphrase, restate, or generate in new form, information that is already classified; then mark the newly developed material consistently with the classification markings that apply to the source information.

b. Derivative classification includes the classification of information based on guidance, which may be either a source document or classification guide. The duplication or reproduction of existing classified information is not derivative classification.

c. Classified information in e-mail messages is subject to all requirements of reference (b) and Part 2001 of reference (z). If an e-mail is transmitted on a classified system, includes a classified attachment and contains no classified information within the body of the e-mail itself, then the e-mail is not a derivative classification decision. The e-mail overall classification must reflect the highest level present in the attachment.

d. The contractor shall ensure that all employees authorized to make derivative classification decisions:

(1) Are identified by name and position, or by personal identifier, on documents they derivatively classify.

(2) Observe and respect original classification decisions.

(3) Carry forward the pertinent classification markings to any newly created documents. For information derivatively classified based on multiple sources, the derivative classifier shall carry forward:

(a) The date or event for declassification that corresponds to the longest period of classification among the sources; and

(b) A listing of the source materials.

(4) Are trained, in accordance with CSA direction, in the proper application of the derivative classification principles, with an emphasis on avoiding over-classification, at least once every 2 years. Training will cover classification levels, duration of classification, identification and markings, classification prohibitions and limitations, sanctions, classification challenges, security classification guides, and information sharing.

(5) Are not authorized to conduct derivative classification until they receive such training.

(6) Are given ready access to the pertinent classification guides and/or guidance necessary to fulfill these important actions.

e. Whenever practicable, derivative classifiers shall use a classified addendum if classified information constitutes a small portion of an otherwise unclassified document.

4-103. Security Classification Guidance. The GCA is responsible for incorporating appropriate security requirements clauses in a classified contract, Invitation for Bid (IFB), Request for Proposal (RFP), Request for Quotation (RFQ), or other solicitation, and for providing the contractor with the security classification guidance needed during the performance of the contract. This guidance is provided to the contractor by the Contract Security Classification Specification. The Contract Security Classification Specification must identify the specific elements of classified information involved in the contract that require security protection.

a. Contractors shall, to the extent practicable, advise and assist in the development of the original Contract Security Classification Specification. It is the contractor's responsibility to understand and apply all aspects of the classification guidance. Users of classification guides are also encouraged to notify the originator of the guide when they acquire information that suggests the need for change in the instructions contained in the guide. Classification guidance is, notwithstanding the contractor's input, the exclusive responsibility of the GCA, and the final determination of the appropriate classification for the information rests with that activity. The Contract Security Classification Specification is a contractual specification necessary for performance on a classified contract. If a classified contract is received without a Contract Security Classification Specification, the contractor shall advise the GCA.

b. The GCA is required to review the existing guidance periodically during the performance stages of the contract and to issue a revised Contract Security Classification Specification when a change occurs to the existing guidance or when additional security classification guidance is needed by the contractor.

c. Upon completion of a classified contract, the contractor must dispose of the classified information according to Chapter 5, Section 7. If the GCA does not advise to the contrary, the contractor may retain classified material for a period of 2 years following completion of the contract. The Contract Security Classification Specification will continue in effect for this 2-year period. If the GCA determines the contractor has a continuing need for the material, the GCA must issue a final Contract Security Classification Specification for the classified contract. A final specification is provided to show the retention period and to provide final disposition instructions for the classified material under the contract.

4-104. Challenges to Classification. Should a contractor believe (a) that information is classified improperly or unnecessarily; or (b) that current security considerations justify downgrading to a lower classification or upgrading to a higher classification; or (c) that the security classification guidance is improper or inadequate, the contractor shall discuss such issues with the pertinent GCA for remedy. If a solution is not forthcoming, and the contractor believes that corrective action is still required, a formal written challenge shall be made to the GCA. Such challenges shall include a description sufficient to identify the issue, the reasons why the contractor believes that corrective action is required, and any recommendations for appropriate corrective action. In any case, the information in question shall be safeguarded as required by this Manual for its assigned or proposed level of classification, whichever is higher, until action is completed. If no written answer is received within 60 days, the CSA should be requested to provide assistance in obtaining a response. If no response is received from the GCA within 120 days, the contractor may also forward the challenge to the Interagency Security Classification Appeals Panel (ISCAP) through the ISOO. The fact that a contractor has initiated such a challenge will not, in any way, serve as a basis for adverse action by the Government. If a contractor believes that adverse action did result from a classification challenge, full details should be furnished promptly to the ISOO for resolution.

4-105. Contractor Developed Information. Whenever a contractor develops an unsolicited proposal or originates information not in the performance of a classified contract, the following rules shall apply:

a. If the information was previously identified as classified, it shall be classified according to an appropriate Contract Security Classification Specification, classification guide, or source document, and marked as required by this Chapter.

b.   If the information was not previously classified, but the contractor believes the information may or should be classified, the contractor should protect the information as though classified at the appropriate level and submit it to the agency that has an interest in the subject matter for a classification determination. In such a case, the following marking, or one that clearly conveys the same meaning, may be used:

CLASSIFICATION DETERMINATION PENDING
Protect as though classified (TOP SECRET,
SECRET, or CONFIDENTIAL).

This marking shall appear conspicuously at least once on the material but no further markings are necessary until a classification determination is received. In addition, contractors are not precluded from marking such material as company-private or proprietary information.   Pending   a   final   classification determination, the contractor should protect the information.   It should be noted however, that reference (b) prohibits classification of information over which the Government has no jurisdiction. To be eligible for classification, the information must: (1) incorporate classified information to which the contractor was given prior access, or (2) the Government must first acquire a proprietary interest in the information.

4-106. Classified Information Appearing in Public Media. The fact that classified information has been made public does not mean that it is automatically declassified.   Contractors   shall   continue   the classification until formally advised to the contrary. Questions   about   the   propriety   of   continued classification in these cases should be brought to the immediate attention of the GCA.

4-107.   Downgrading or Declassifying Classified Information.   Information   is   downgraded   or declassified based on the loss of sensitivity of the information due to the passage of time or on occurrence   of   a   specific   event.   Contractors downgrade or declassify information based on the guidance   provided   in   a   Contract   Security Classification   Specification   or   upon   formal notification.   If material is marked for automatic declassification, the contractor shall seek guidance from the GCA prior to taking any action. Downgrading or declassifying actions constitute implementation of a directed action rather than an exercise of the authority for deciding the change or cancellation of the classification.   At the time the material is actually downgraded or declassified, the action to update records and change the classification markings   shall   be   initiated   and   performed. Declassification is not automatically an approval for public disclosure.

Section 2. Marking Requirements

4-200. General. Physically marking classified information with appropriate classification markings serves to warn and inform holders of the information of the degree of protection required. Other notations facilitate downgrading, declassification, and aid in derivative classification actions. Therefore, it is essential that all classified information and material be marked to clearly convey to the holder the level of classification assigned, the portions that contain or reveal classified information, the period of time protection is required, the identity (by name and position or personal identifier) of the classifier, the source(s) for derivative classification, and any other notations required for protection of the information.

4-201. Marking Requirements for Information and Material. As a general rule, the markings specified in paragraphs 4-202 through 4-208 are required for all classified information regardless of the form in which it appears. Some material, such as documents, letters, and reports, can be easily marked with the required markings. Marking other material, such as equipment, IS media, and slides may be more difficult due to size or other physical characteristics. Since the primary purpose of the markings is to alert the holder that the information requires special protection, it is essential that all classified material be marked to the fullest extent possible to ensure the necessary safeguarding.

4-202. Identification Markings. All classified material shall be marked to show the name and address of the contractor responsible for its preparation, the identity of the person (by name and position or personal identifier) responsible for each derivative classification action, and the date of preparation. These markings are required on the face of all classified documents.

4-203. Overall Markings. The highest level of classified information contained in a document is its overall marking. The overall marking shall be conspicuously marked or stamped at the top and bottom on the outside of the front cover, on the title page, on the first page, and on the outside of the back. All copies of classified documents shall also bear the required markings. Overall markings shall be stamped, printed, etched, written, engraved, painted, or affixed by means of a tag, sticker, decal, or similar device on classified material other than documents, and on containers of such material, if possible. If marking the material or container is not practical, written notification of the markings shall be furnished to recipients.

4-204. Page Markings. Interior pages of classified documents shall be conspicuously marked or stamped at the top and bottom with the highest classification of the information appearing thereon, or the designation UNCLASSIFIED, if all the information on the particular page is UNCLASSIFIED. Alternatively, the overall classification of the document may be conspicuously marked or stamped at the top and bottom of each interior page, when necessary to achieve production efficiency, and the particular information to which classification is assigned is adequately identified by portion markings according to paragraph 4-206.

4-205. Component Markings. The major components of complex documents are likely to be used separately. In such cases, each major component shall be marked as a separate document. Examples include: (a) each annex, appendix, or similar component of a plan, program, or project description; (b) attachments and appendices to a letter; and (c) each major part of a report. If an entire major component is UNCLASSIFIED, the first page of the component may be marked at the top and bottom with the designation UNCLASSIFIED and a statement included, such as: "All portions of this (annex, appendix, etc.) are UNCLASSIFIED." When this method of marking is used, no further markings are required on the unclassified major component.

4-206. Portion Markings.

a. Each section, part, paragraph, or similar portion of a document containing classified information shall be marked to show the highest level of its classification and any applicable control markings, or the portion is unclassified. Portions of documents shall be marked in a manner that eliminates doubt as to which of its portions contain or reveal classified information. Classification levels of portions of a document shall be shown by the appropriate classification symbol placed immediately before the portion to which it applies. For paragraphs or subparagraphs beginning with numbers, letters or symbols such as bullets, place the portion marking after the number, letter or bullet and before the text. In marking portions, the parenthetical symbols (TS) for TOP SECRET, (S) for SECRET, (C) for CONFIDENTIAL, and (U) for UNCLASSIFIED shall be used as well as the authorized abbreviation(s) for any applicable control markings.

b. Illustrations, photographs, figures, graphs, drawings, charts, or similar portions contained in classified documents shall be marked clearly to show their classified or unclassified status. These classification markings shall be prominent and placed within or contiguous to such a portion. Captions of such portions shall be marked on the basis of their content.

4-207. Subject and Title Markings. Unclassified subjects and titles shall be selected for classified documents, if possible. A subject or title shall be marked with the appropriate symbol placed immediately before the item, which shall reflect the classification of the title, not the content of the document.

4-208. Markings for Derivatively Classified Documents. All classified information shall be marked to reflect the source of the classification and declassification instructions. Documents shall show the required information either on the cover, first page, title page, or in another prominent position. Other material shall show the required information on the material itself or, if not practical, in related or accompanying documentation.

a. **"CLASSIFIED BY" Line.** The purpose of the "Classified By" line is to identify the person who applies derivative classification markings for the document. If not otherwise evident, the line will include the contractor and, where available, the office of origin will be identified and follow the name and position or personal identifier of the derivative classifier.

b. **"DERIVED FROM" Line.** The purpose of the "Derived From" line is to link the derivative classification applied to the material by the contractor and the source document(s) or classification guide(s) under which it was classified. In completing the "Derived From" line, the contractor shall identify the applicable guidance that authorizes the classification of the material. Normally this will be a security classification guide listed on the Contract Security Classification Specification or a source document. When identifying a classification guide on the "Derived From" line, the guide's title or number, issuing agency, and date shall be included. Many Contract Security Classification Specifications cite more than one classification guide and/or the contractor is extracting information from more than one classified source document. In these cases, the contractor may use the phrase "multiple sources." When the phrase "multiple sources" is used, the contractor shall include a listing of the source materials in, or attached to, each derivatively classified document. This listing may take the form of a bibliography identifying the applicable classification sources.

c. **"DECLASSIFY ON" Line.** The purpose of the "Declassify On" line is to provide declassification instructions appropriate for the material. When completing this line, the contractor shall use the information specified in the Contract Security Classification Specification or classification guide furnished with a classified contract. Or, the contractor shall carry forward the duration instruction from the source document or classification guide (e.g., date or event). When the source is marked "Original Agency's Determination Required" (OADR), "X1 through X8", Manual Review (MR), "DNI Only," "DCI Only," or contains any other no longer valid declassification instruction, the "Declassify On" line shall be marked with a date that is 25 years from the date of the source document, unless other guidance has been provided by the OCA. When a document is classified derivatively on the basis of more than one source document or more than one element of a classification guide, the "Declassify On" line shall reflect the longest duration of any of its sources. Material containing RD or FRD shall not have a "Declassify On" line unless co-mingled with national security information subject to reference (b).

d. **"DOWNGRADE TO" Line.** When downgrading instructions are contained in the Contract Security Classification Specification, classification guide or source document a "Downgrade To" line will be included. When completing this line, the contractor shall insert SECRET or CONFIDENTIAL and an effective date or event. The markings used to show this information are:

DERIVED FROM

DOWNGRADE TO   ON

DECLASSIFY ON

4-209. Documents Generated Under Previous E.O.s. Documents classified under previous E.O.s need not be re-marked to comply with the marking requirements of reference (b).

a. Classified material originated under recent E.O.s contains overall, portion, paragraph, and appropriate downgrading and declassification markings that will provide sufficient guidance for the classification of extracted information. However, classified material originated under previous E.O.s may not have these markings. If the source document does not contain portion markings, the overall classification of the source document shall be used for the extracted information in the new document.

b. The classification markings for a source document are the responsibility of the originator and not the contractor extracting the information. Contractors are encouraged to contact the originator to avoid improper or unnecessary classification of material.

4-210. Marking Special Types of Material. The following procedures are for marking special types of material, but are not all inclusive. The intent of the markings is to ensure that the classification of the item, regardless of its form, is clear to the holder.

a. **Files, Folders, or Groups of Documents.** Files, folders, binders, envelopes, and other items containing classified documents, when not in secure storage, shall be conspicuously marked with the highest classification of any classified item included in the group. Cover sheets may be used for this purpose.

b. **E-mail and other Electronic Messages.** Electronically transmitted messages shall be marked in the same manner required for other documents except as noted. The overall classification of the message shall be the first item of information in the text and shall be displayed at the top and bottom of each message. A "Classified By" line, a "Derived From" line, a "Declassify On" line, and portion markings are required on messages. E-mail transmitted on or prepared for transmission on classified systems or networks shall be configured to display:

(1) The overall classification at the top and bottom of the body of each message; the overall classification marking string for the e-mail will reflect the classification of the header and body of the message, including the subject line, the text of the e-mail, a classified signature block, attachments, included messages, and any other information conveyed in the body of the e-mail; classified e-mail will be portion marked.

(2) When forwarding or replying to an e-mail, contractors shall ensure that the classification markings reflect the overall classification and declassification instructions for the entire string of e-mails and attachments. This includes any newly drafted material, material received from previous senders, and any attachments.

(3) When messages are printed by an automated system, all markings may be applied by that system, provided the classification markings are clearly distinguished from the printed text. The markings required by paragraph 4-208 shall be included after the signature block, but before the overall classification marking at the end of the e-mail. The last line of the message shall be the overall classification of the e-mail.

c. **Microforms.** Microforms contain images or text in sizes too small to be read by the unaided eye. The applicable markings shall be conspicuously marked on the microform medium or its container to be readable by the unaided eye. These markings shall also be included on the image so that when the image is enlarged and displayed or printed, the markings will be conspicuous and readable. Further markings and handling shall be as appropriate for the particular microform involved.

d. **Translations.** Translations of U.S. classified information into a language other than English shall be marked to show the United States as the country of origin, with the appropriate U.S. markings and the foreign language equivalent.

4-211. Marking Transmittal Documents. A transmittal document shall be marked with the highest level of classified information and applicable control markings, if any, contained in the document and with an appropriate notation to indicate its classification when the enclosures are removed. An unclassified document that transmits a classified document as an attachment shall bear a notation substantially as follows: "Unclassified when Separated from Classified Enclosures." A classified transmittal that transmits higher classified information shall be marked with a notation substantially as follows: "CONFIDENTIAL (or SECRET) when Separated from Enclosures." In addition, a classified transmittal itself must bear all the classification markings required for a classified document.

4-212. Marking Wholly Unclassified Material. Normally, wholly UNCLASSIFIED material will not be marked or stamped UNCLASSIFIED unless it is essential to convey to a recipient of such material that (a) the material has been examined specifically with a view to impose a security classification and has been determined not to require classification; or (b) the material has been reviewed and has been determined to no longer require classification and it is declassified.

4-213. Marking Compilations. In some instances, certain information that would otherwise be unclassified when standing alone may require classification when combined or associated with other unclassified information. The determination that information requires classification by compilation will be based on specific guidance regarding compilation provided in a Contract Security Classification Specification or a security classification guide. If specific guidance is absent, the contractor will obtain written guidance from the applicable GCA. When classification is required to protect a compilation of such information, the overall classification assigned to the compilation shall be conspicuously affixed. The reason for classifying the compilation shall be stated at an appropriate location at or near the beginning of the compilation. Any unclassified portions will be portion marked (U), while the overall markings will reflect the classification of the compiled information, even if all the portions are marked (U).

4-214. Working Papers. Working papers containing classified information shall be dated when created; marked with the highest classification of any information contained in them; protected at that level; and if otherwise appropriate, destroyed when no longer needed. Working papers shall be controlled and marked in the same manner prescribed for a finished document at the same classification level if released outside of the facility, filed permanently, or retained for more than 180 days from the date of the origin, filed permanently, e-mailed within or released outside the originating activity.

4-215. Marking Miscellaneous Material. Material developed in connection with the handling, processing, production, storage and utilization of classified information shall be handled in a manner that ensures adequate protection of the classified information involved and shall be destroyed at the earliest practical time, unless a requirement exists to retain such material. There is no requirement to mark such material.

4-216. Marking Training Material. Unclassified documents or materials that are created to simulate or demonstrate classified documents or material shall be clearly marked to indicate the actual UNCLASSIFIED status of the information. For example: SECRET FOR TRAINING PURPOSES ONLY, OTHERWISE UNCLASSIFIED or UNCLASSIFIED SAMPLE, or a similar marking may be used.

4-217. Downgrading or Declassification Actions. When documents or material that have been downgraded or declassified are removed from storage for use or for transmittal outside the facility, they shall be re-marked according to paragraph a or b below. If the volume of material is such that prompt re-marking of each classified item cannot be accomplished without unduly interfering with operations, a downgrading and declassification notice may be attached to the inside of the file drawers or other storage container instead of the re-marking otherwise required. Each notice shall specify the authority for the downgrading or declassification action, the date of the action, and the storage container to which it applies. When documents or other material subject to downgrading or declassification are withdrawn from the container solely for transfer to another, or when the container is transferred from one place to another, the transfer may be made without re-marking if the notice is attached to the new container or remains with each shipment.

a. Prior to taking any action to downgrade or declassify information, the contractor shall seek guidance from the GCA. If such action is approved, all old classification markings shall be canceled and the new markings substituted, whenever practical. In the case of documents, as a minimum the outside of the front cover, the title page, the first page, and the outside of the back shall reflect the new classification markings, or the designation UNCLASSIFIED. Other material shall be re-marked by the most practical method for the type of material involved to ensure that it is clear to the holder what level of classification is assigned to the material.

b. When contractors are notified of downgrading or declassification actions that are contrary to the markings shown on the material, the material shall be re-marked to indicate the change. In addition, the material shall be marked to indicate the authority for the action, the date of the action, and the identity of the person or contractor taking the action. Other holders shall be notified if further dissemination has been made by the contractor.

4-218. Upgrading Action

a. When a notice is received to upgrade material to a higher level, for example from CONFIDENTIAL to SECRET, the new markings shall be immediately entered on the material according to the notice to upgrade, and all the superseded markings shall be obliterated. The authority for and the date of the upgrading action shall be entered on the material. Other holders shall be notified as appropriate if further dissemination of the material has been made by the contractor.

b. The contractor's notice shall not be classified unless the notice contains additional information warranting classification. In the case of material which was inadvertently released as UNCLASSIFIED, the contractor's notice shall be classified CONFIDENTIAL, unless it contains additional information warranting a higher classification. The notice shall cite the applicable Contract Security Classification Specification or other classification guide on the "Derived From" line and be marked with an appropriate declassification instruction.

4-219. Inadvertent Release. If classified material is inadvertently distributed outside the facility without the proper classification assigned to it, or without any markings to identify the material as classified, the contractor shall, as appropriate:

a. Determine whether all holders of the material are cleared and authorized access to it.

b. Determine whether control of the material has been lost.

c. If recipients are cleared for access to the material, promptly provide written notice to all holders of the proper classification to be assigned. If control of the material has been lost, if all copies cannot be accounted for, or if unauthorized personnel have had access to it, report the compromise to the CSA.

4-220. Marking requirements for transfers of defense articles to AUS or the United Kingdom (UK). Marking requirements for transfers of defense articles to AUS or UK without a license or other written authorization are located in Chapter 10, Section 8 of this Manual.

4-221. Comingling of Restricted Data and Formerly Restricted Data. To the greatest degree possible, do not comingle RD and FRD in the same document with information classified pursuant to reference (b). When mixing can't be avoided, the requirements of references (b) and (z) must be met.

CHAPTER 5
Safeguarding Classified Information

Section 1. General Safeguarding Requirements

5-100. General. Contractors shall be responsible for safeguarding classified information in their custody or under their control. Individuals are responsible for safeguarding classified information entrusted to them. The extent of protection afforded classified information shall be sufficient to reasonably foreclose the possibility of its loss or compromise.

5-101. Safeguarding Oral Discussions. Contractors shall ensure that all cleared personnel are aware of the prohibition against discussing classified information over unsecured telephones, in public conveyances or places, or in any other manner that permits interception by unauthorized persons.

5-102. End of Day Security Checks

a. Contractors that store classified material shall establish a system of security checks at the close of each working day to ensure that all classified material and security repositories have been appropriately secured.

b. Contractors that operate multiple work shifts shall perform the security checks at the end of the last working shift in which classified material was removed from storage for use. The checks are not required during continuous 24-hour operations.

5-103. Perimeter Controls. Contractors authorized to store classified material shall establish and maintain a system to deter and detect unauthorized introduction or removal of classified material from their facility. The objective is to discourage the introduction or removal of classified material without proper authority. If the unauthorized introduction or removal of classified material can be reasonably foreclosed through technical means, which are

encouraged, no further controls are necessary. Personnel who have a legitimate need to remove or transport classified material should be provided appropriate authorization for passing through designated entry/exit points. The fact that persons who enter or depart the facility are subject to an inspection of their personal effects shall be conspicuously posted at all pertinent entries and exits.

a. All persons who enter or exit the facility shall be subject to an inspection of their personal effects, except under circumstances where the possibility of access to classified material is remote. Inspections shall be limited to buildings or areas where classified work is being performed. Inspections are not required of wallets, change purses, clothing, cosmetics cases, or other objects of an unusually personal nature.

b. The extent, frequency, and location of inspections shall be accomplished in a manner consistent with contractual obligations and operational efficiency. Inspections may be done using any appropriate random sampling technique. Contractors are encouraged to seek legal advice during the formulation of implementing procedures and to surface significant problems to the CSA.

5-104. Emergency Procedures. Contractors shall develop procedures for safeguarding classified material in emergency situations. The procedures shall be as simple and practical as possible and should be adaptable to any type of emergency that may reasonably arise. Contractors shall promptly report to the CSA any emergency situation that renders the facility incapable of safeguarding classified material.

Section 2. Control and Accountability

5-200. Policy. Contractors shall establish an information management system to protect and control the classified information in their possession. Contractors shall ensure that classified information in their custody is used or retained only for a lawful and authorized U.S. Government purpose. The U.S. Government reserves the right to retrieve its classified material or to cause appropriate disposition of the material by the contractor. The information management system employed by the contractor shall be capable of facilitating such retrieval and disposition in a reasonable period of time.

5-201. Accountability for TOP SECRET

a. TOP SECRET control officials shall be designated to receive, transmit, and maintain access and accountability records for TOP SECRET information. An inventory shall be conducted annually unless written relief is granted by the GCA.

b. The transmittal of TOP SECRET information shall be covered by a continuous receipt system both within and outside the facility.

c. Each item of TOP SECRET material shall be numbered in series. The copy number shall be placed on TOP SECRET documents and on all associated transaction documents.

5-202. Receiving Classified Material. Procedures shall be established to ensure that classified material, regardless of delivery method, is received directly by authorized personnel. The material shall be examined for evidence of tampering and the classified contents shall be checked against the receipt. Discrepancies in the contents of a package or absence of a receipt for TOP SECRET and SECRET material shall be reported promptly to the sender. If the shipment is in order, the receipt shall be signed and returned to the sender. If a receipt is included with CONFIDENTIAL material, it shall be signed and returned to the sender.

5-203. Generation of Classified Material

a. A record of TOP SECRET material produced by the contractor shall be made when the material is: (1) completed as a finished document, (2) retained for more than 180 days after creation, regardless of the stage of development, or (3) transmitted outside the facility.

b. Classified working papers generated by the contractor in the preparation of a finished document shall be: (1) dated when created, (2) marked with its overall classification and with the annotation "WORKING PAPERS", and (3) destroyed when no longer needed. Working papers shall be marked in the same manner prescribed for a finished document at the same classification level if released outside the facility, or retained for more than 180 days from the date of origin.

Section 3. Storage and Storage Equipment

5-300. General. This section describes the uniform requirements for the physical protection of classified material in the custody of contractors. Where these requirements are not appropriate for protecting specific types or forms of classified material, compensatory provisions shall be developed and approved by the CSA. Nothing in this Manual shall be construed to contradict or inhibit compliance with the law or building codes. Cognizant security officials shall work to meet appropriate security needs according to the intent of this Manual and at acceptable cost.

5-301. GSA Storage Equipment. GSA establishes and publishes uniform standards, specifications, and supply schedules for units and key-operated and combination padlocks suitable for the storage and protection of classified information. Manufacturers and prices of storage equipment approved by the GSA are listed in the Federal Supply Schedule (P55) catalog (FSC GROUP 71-Pan II). Copies of specifications and schedules may be obtained from any regional office of the GSA.

5-302. TOP SECRET Storage. TOP SECRET material shall be stored in a GSA-approved security container, an approved vault, or an approved closed area with supplemental controls.

5-303. SECRET Storage. SECRET material shall be stored in a GSA-approved security container, an approved vault, or closed area. Supplemental controls are required for storage in closed areas.

5-304. CONFIDENTIAL Storage. CONFIDENTIAL material shall be stored in the same manner as TOP SECRET or SECRET material except that no supplemental protection is required.

5-305. Restricted Areas. When it is necessary to control access to classified material in an open area during working hours, a restricted area may be established. A restricted area will normally become necessary when it is impractical or impossible to protect classified material because of its size, quantity or other unusual characteristic. The restricted area shall have a clearly defined perimeter, but physical barriers are not required. Personnel within the area shall be responsible for challenging all persons who may lack appropriate access authority. All classified material will be secured during non-working hours in approved repositories or secured using other methods approved by the CSA.

5-306. Closed Areas. Due to the size and nature of the classified material, or for operational necessity, it may be necessary to construct closed areas for storage because GSA-approved containers or vaults are unsuitable or impractical. Closed areas must be constructed in accordance with section 8 of this chapter. Access to closed areas must be controlled to preclude unauthorized access. This may be accomplished through the use of a cleared person or by a supplanting access control device or system. Access shall be limited to authorized persons who have an appropriate security clearance and a need-to-know for the classified material/information within the area. Persons without the appropriate level of clearance and/or need to know shall be escorted at all times by an authorized person where inadvertent or unauthorized exposure to classified information cannot otherwise be effectively prevented. Closed areas storing TOP SECRET and SECRET material shall be accorded supplemental protection during non-working hours. During non-working hours and during working hours when the area is unattended, admittance to the area shall be controlled by locked entrances and exits secured by either an approved built-in combination lock or an approved combination or key-operated padlock. It is not necessary to activate the supplemental controls during working hours. Doors secured from the inside with a panic bolt (for example, actuated by a panic bar, a dead bolt, a rigid wood or metal bar) or other means approved by the CSA, will not require additional locking devices.

a. Contractors shall develop and implement procedures to ensure the structural integrity of closed areas above false ceilings and below raised floors.

b. Open shelf or bin storage of SECRET and CONFIDENTIAL documents in closed areas requires CSA approval. For SECRET material only areas protected by an approved Intrusion Detection System (IDS) will qualify for such approval. Open shelf or bin storage of TOP SECRET documents is not permitted.

c. The CSA and the contractor shall agree on the need to establish, and the extent of, closed areas prior to the award of the contract, when possible, or when the need for such areas becomes apparent during contract performance.

d. The CSA may grant self-approval authority to

the FSO for closed area approvals provided the FSO meets specified qualification criteria as determined by the CSA.

5-307. Supplemental Protection

a. IDS as described in section 9 of this Chapter shall be used as supplemental protection.

b. Security guards approved as supplemental protection prior to January 1, 1995, may continue to be utilized. When guards are authorized, the schedule of patrol is 2 hours for TOP SECRET material and 4 hours for SECRET material.

c. GSA-approved security containers and approved vaults secured with a locking mechanism meeting Federal Specification FF-L-2740 do not require supplemental protection when the CSA has determined that the GSA-approved security container or approved vault is located in an area of the facility with security-in-depth.

5-308. Protection of Combinations to Security Containers, Cabinets, Vaults and Closed Areas. Only a minimum number of authorized persons shall have knowledge of combinations to authorized storage containers. Containers shall bear no external markings indicating the level of classified material authorized for storage.

a. A record of the names of persons having knowledge of the combination shall be maintained.

b. Security containers, vaults, cabinets, and other authorized storage containers shall be kept locked when not under the direct supervision of an authorized person entrusted with the contents.

c. The combination shall be safeguarded in accordance with the highest classification of the material authorized for storage in the container.

d. If a record is made of a combination, the record shall be marked with the highest classification of material authorized for storage in the container.

5-309. Changing Combinations. Combinations shall be changed by a person authorized access to the contents of the container, or by the FSO or his or her designee. Combinations shall be changed as follows:

a. The initial use of an approved container or lock for the protection of classified material.

b. The termination of employment of any person having knowledge of the combination, or when the clearance granted to any such person has been withdrawn, suspended, or revoked.

c. The compromise or suspected compromise of a container or its combination, or discovery of a container left unlocked and unattended.

d. At other times when considered necessary by the FSO or CSA.

5-310. Supervision of Keys and Padlocks. Use of key-operated padlocks are subject to the following requirements: (i) a key and lock custodian shall be appointed to ensure proper custody and handling of keys and locks used for protection of classified material; (ii) a key and lock control register shall be maintained to identify keys for each lock and their current location and custody; (iii) keys and locks shall be audited each month; (iv) keys shall be inventoried with each change of custody; (v) keys shall not be removed from the premises; (vi) keys and spare locks shall be protected equivalent to the level of classified material involved; (vii) locks shall be changed or rotated at least annually and shall be replaced after loss or compromise of their operable keys; and (viii) making master keys is prohibited.

5-311. Repair of Approved Containers. Repairs, maintenance, or other actions that affect the physical integrity of a security container approved for storage of classified information shall be accomplished only by appropriately cleared or continuously escorted personnel specifically trained in approved methods of maintenance and repair of containers. Repair procedures may be obtained from the CSA.

a. An approved security container is considered to have been restored to its original state of security integrity if all damaged or altered parts are replaced with manufacturer's replacement or identical cannibalized parts.

b. The repairer will provide a signed and dated certification for each repaired container that describes the method of repair used; certifications will be kept on file by the contractor.

5-312. Supplanting Access Control Systems or Devices. Automated access control systems and electronic, mechanical, or electromechanical devices which meet the criteria stated in paragraphs 5-313 and 5-314, below, may be used to supplant contractor-authorized personnel or guards to control admittance to closed areas during working hours. Approval of the FSO is required before effecting the installation of a supplanting access control device to meet a requirement of this Manual.

5-313. Automated Access Control Systems. The automated access control system must be capable of identifying the individual entering the area and authenticating that person's authority to enter the area.

a. Manufacturers of automated access control equipment or devices must assure in writing that their system will meet the following standards before FSOs may favorably consider such systems for protection of classified information:

(1) Chances of an unauthorized individual gaining access through normal operation of the equipment are no more than one in ten thousand.

(2) Chances of an authorized individual being rejected for access through normal operation of the equipment are no more than one in one thousand.

b. Identification of individuals entering the area can be obtained by an identification (ID) badge or card, or by personal identity.

(1) The ID badge or card must use embedded sensors, integrated circuits, magnetic stripes or other means of encoding data that identifies the facility and the individual to whom the card is issued.

(2) Personal identity verification identifies the individual requesting access by some unique personal characteristic, such as, (a) fingerprint, (b) hand geometry, (c) handwriting. (d) retina, or (e) voice recognition.

c. In conjunction with an ID badge or card or personal identity verification, a personal identification number (PIN) is required. The PIN must be separately entered into the system by each individual using a keypad device. The PIN shall consist of four or more digits, randomly selected with no known or logical association with the individual. The PIN must be changed when it is believed to have been subjected to compromise.

d. Authentication of the individual's authorization to enter the area must be accomplished within the system by comparing the inputs from the ID badge or card or the personal identity verification device and the keypad with an electronic database of individuals authorized into the area. A procedure must be established for removal of the individual's authorization to enter the area upon reassignment, transfer or termination, or when the individual's PCL is suspended or revoked.

e. Locations where access transactions are, or can be displayed, and where authorization data, card encoded data and personal identification or verification data is input, stored, displayed, or recorded must be protected.

f. Control panels, card readers, keypads, communication or interface devices located outside the entrance to a closed area shall have tamper-resistant enclosures, be securely fastened to a wall or other structure, be protected by a tamper alarm, or secured with an approved combination padlock. Control panels located within a closed area shall require only a minimal degree of physical security protection sufficient to preclude unauthorized access to the mechanism. Where areas containing TOP SECRET information are involved, tamper alarm protection is mandatory.

g. Systems that utilize transmission lines to carry access authorization, personal identification, or verification data between devices/equipment located outside the closed area shall receive circuit protection equal to or greater than that specified as Grade A by Underwriters Laboratories (UL).

h. Access to records and information concerning encoded ID data and PINs shall be restricted to individuals cleared at the same level as the highest classified information contained within the specific area or areas in which ID data or PINs are utilized. Access to identification or authorization data, operating system software or any identifying data associated with the access control system shall be limited to the least number of personnel possible. Such data or software shall be kept secured when unattended.

i. Records reflecting active assignments of ID badges/cards, PINs, levels of access, and similar system-related records shall be maintained. Records concerning personnel removed from the system shall be retained for 90 days.

j. Personnel entering or leaving an area shall be required to immediately secure the entrance or exit point. Authorized personnel who permit another individual entrance into the area are responsible for confirming the individual's PCL and need-to-know. During shift changes and emergency situations, if the door remains open, admittance shall be controlled by a contractor-authorized person or guard stationed to supervise the entrance to the area.

5-314. Electronic, Mechanical, or Electro-mechanical Devices. Provided the classified material within the closed area is no higher than SECRET, electronic, mechanical, or electro-mechanical devices that meet the criteria below may be used to supplant contractor authorized personnel or guards to control admittance to closed areas during working hours. Devices may be used that operate by either a push-button combination that activates the locking device or by a control card used in conjunction with a push-button combination, thereby excluding any system that operates solely by the use of a control card.

a. The electronic control panel containing the mechanism by which the combination is set may be located inside or outside the closed area. When located outside the closed area, the control panel shall be securely fastened or attached to the perimeter barrier of the area and secured by an approved combination padlock. If the control panel is located within the closed area, it shall require only a minimal degree of physical security designed to preclude

unauthorized access to the mechanism.

b. The control panel shall be installed in a manner that precludes an unauthorized person in the immediate vicinity from observing the selection of the correct combination of the push buttons, or have a shielding device mounted.

c. The selection and setting of the combination shall be accomplished by an employee of the contractor who is authorized to enter the area. The combination shall be changed as specified in paragraph 5-309. The combination shall be classified and safeguarded in accordance with the classification of the highest classified material within the closed area.

d. Electrical gear, wiring included, or mechanical links (cables, rods, etc.) shall be accessible only from inside the area, or shall be secured within a protective covering to preclude surreptitious manipulation of components.

e. Personnel entering or leaving the area shall be required to secure the entrance or exit point immediately. Authorized personnel who permit another individual entrance into the area are responsible for confirming the individual's PCL and need-to-know. During shift changes and emergency situations, if the door remains open, admittance shall be controlled by a contractor-authorized person or guard stationed to supervise the entrance to the area.

Section 4. Transmission

5-400.   General.   Classified material shall be transmitted outside the contractor's facility in a manner that prevents loss or unauthorized access.

5-401. Preparation and Receipting

a. Classified information to be transmitted outside of a facility shall be enclosed in opaque inner and outer covers. The inner cover shall be a sealed wrapper or envelope plainly marked with the assigned classification and addresses of both sender and addressee. The outer cover shall be sealed and addressed with no identification of the classification of its contents. A receipt shall be attached to or enclosed in the inner cover, except that CONFIDENTIAL information shall require a receipt only if the sender deems it necessary. The receipt shall identify the sender, the addressee and the document, but shall contain no classified information. It shall be signed by the recipient and returned to the sender.

b. A suspense system will be established to track transmitted documents until a signed copy of the receipt is returned.

c. When the material is of a size, weight, or nature that precludes the use of envelopes, the materials used for packaging shall be of such strength and durability to ensure the necessary protection while the material is in transit.

5-402. TOP SECRET Transmission Outside a Facility. Written authorization of the GCA is required to transmit TOP SECRET information outside of the facility. TOP SECRET material may be transmitted by the following methods within and directly between the United States and its territorial areas.

a. The Defense Courier Service, if authorized by the GCA.

b. A designated courier or escort cleared for access to TOP SECRET information.

c. By electrical means over CSA-approved secured communications security circuits, provided such transmission conforms with this Manual, the telecommunications security provisions of the contract, or as otherwise authorized by the GCA.

5-403. SECRET Transmission Outside a Facility. SECRET material may be transmitted by one of the following methods within and directly between the United States and its territorial areas:

a. By the methods established for TOP SECRET.

b. U.S. Postal Service Express Mail and U.S. Postal Service Registered Mail. NOTE: The "Waiver of Signature and Indemnity" block on the U.S. Postal Service Express Mail Label 11-B may not be executed and the use of external (street side) express mail collection boxes is prohibited.

c. A cleared commercial carrier.

d.   A cleared commercial messenger service engaged in the intercity/local area delivery (same day delivery only) of classified material.

e. A commercial delivery company, approved by the CSA, that provides nation-wide, overnight service with computer tracking and reporting features. Such companies need not be security cleared.

f. Other methods as directed in writing by the GCA.

5-404. CONFIDENTIAL Transmission Outside a Facility. CONFIDENTIAL material shall be transmitted by the methods established for SECRET material, except that a commercial carrier does not have to be cleared, or by U.S. Postal Service Certified Mail.

5-405. Transmission Outside the United States and Its Territorial Areas. Classified material may be transmitted to a U.S. Government activity outside the United States or a U.S. territory only under the provisions of a classified contract or with the written authorization of the GCA.

a. TOP SECRET material may be transmitted by the Defense Courier Service, Department of State Courier System, or a courier service authorized by the GCA.

b. SECRET and CONFIDENTIAL material may be transmitted by: (1) registered mail through U.S. Army, Navy, or Air Force postal facilities; (2) by an appropriately cleared contractor employee; (3) by a U.S. civil service employee or military person, who has been designated by the GCA; (4) by U.S. and Canadian registered mail with registered mail receipt to and from Canada and via a U.S. or a Canadian government activity; or (5) as authorized by the GCA.

5-406. Addressing Classified Material. Mail or shipments containing classified material shall be addressed to the Commander or approved classified mailing address of a Federal activity or to a cleared contractor using the name and classified mailing address of the facility. An individual's name shall not appear on the outer cover. This does not prevent the use of office code letters, numbers, or phrases in an attention line to aid in internal routing.

a. When it is necessary to direct SECRET or CONFIDENTIAL material to the attention of a particular individual, other than as prescribed below, the identity of the intended recipient shall be indicated on an attention line placed in the letter of transmittal or on the inner container or wrapper.

b. When addressing SECRET or CONFIDENTIAL material to an individual operating as an independent consultant, or to any facility at which only one employee is assigned, the outer container shall specify: "TO BE OPENED BY ADDRESSEE ONLY" and be annotated: "POSTMASTER-DO NOT FORWARD. IF UNDELIVERABLE TO ADDRESSEE, RETURN TO SENDER."

5-407. Transmission Within a Facility. Classified material may be transmitted within a facility without single or double-wrapping provided adequate measures are taken to protect the material against unauthorized disclosure.

5-408. SECRET Transmission by Commercial Carrier. SECRET material may be shipped by a cleared commercial carrier that has been approved by the CSA to transport SECRET shipments. Commercial carriers may be used only within and between the 48 contiguous States and the District of Columbia or wholly within Alaska, Hawaii, or a U.S. territory. When the services of a commercial carrier are required, the contractor, as consignor, shall be responsible for the following:

a. The material shall be prepared for transmission to afford additional protection against pilferage, theft, and compromise as follows.

(1) The material shall be shipped in hardened containers unless specifically authorized otherwise by the contracting agency.

(2) Carrier equipment shall be sealed by the contractor or a representative of the carrier when there is a full carload, a full truckload, exclusive use of the vehicle, or when a closed and locked compartment of the carrier's equipment is used. The seals shall be numbered and the numbers indicated on all copies of the bill of lading (BL). When seals are used, the BL shall be annotated substantially as follows: DO NOT BREAK SEALS EXCEPT IN CASE OF EMERGENCY OR UPON PRIOR AUTHORITY OF THE CONSIGNOR OR CONSIGNEE. IF FOUND BROKEN OR IF BROKEN FOR EMERGENCY REASONS, APPLY CARRIER'S SEALS AS SOON AS POSSIBLE AND IMMEDIATELY NOTIFY BOTH THE CONSIGNOR AND THE CONSIGNEE.

(3) For DoD contractors the notation "Protective Security Service Required" shall be reflected on all copies of the BL. The BL will be maintained in a suspense file to follow-up on overdue or delayed shipments.

b. The contractor shall utilize a qualified carrier selected by the U.S. Government that will provide a single-line service from point of origin to destination, when such service is available, or by such transshipping procedures as may be specified by the U.S. Government.

c. The contractor shall request routing instructions, including designation of a qualified carrier, from the GCA or designated representative (normally the government transportation officer). The request shall specify that the routing instructions are required for the shipment of SECRET material and include the point of origin and point of destination.

d. The contractor shall notify the consignee (including U.S. Government transshipping activity) of the nature of the shipment, the means of the shipment, numbers of the seals, if used, and the anticipated time and date of arrival by separate communication at least 24 hours in advance (or immediately on dispatch if transit time is less than 24 hours) of the arrival of the shipment. This notification shall be addressed to the appropriate organizational entity and not to an individual. Request that the consignee activity (including a military transshipping activity) notify the consignor of any shipment not received within 48 hours after the estimated time of arrival indicated by the consignor.

e. In addition, the contractor shall annotate the BL: "CARRIER TO NOTIFY THE CONSIGNOR AND CONSIGNEE (Telephone Numbers) IMMEDIATELY IF SHIPMENT IS DELAYED

BECAUSE OF AN ACCIDENT OR INCIDENT. IF NEITHER CAN BE REACHED, CONTACT (Enter appropriate HOTLINE Number). USE HOTLINE NUMBER TO OBTAIN SAFE HAVEN OR REFUGE INSTRUCTIONS IN THE EVENT OF A CIVIL DISORDER, NATURAL DISASTER, CARRIER STRIKE OR OTHER EMERGENCY."

5-409. CONFIDENTIAL Transmission by Commercial Carrier. CONFIDENTIAL material may be shipped by a CSA or GCA-approved commercial carrier. For DoD contractors a commercial carrier authorized by law, regulatory body, or regulation to provide the required transportation service shall be used when a determination has been made by the Surface Deployment and Distribution Command (SDDC) (formerly known as the Military Traffic Management Command) that the carrier has a tariff, government tender, agreement, or contract that provides Constant Surveillance Service. Commercial carriers may be used only within and between the 48 contiguous states and the District of Columbia or wholly within Alaska, Hawaii, or a U.S. territory. An FCL is not required for the commercial carrier. The contractor, as consignor, shall:

a. Utilize containers of such strength and durability as to provide security protection to prevent items from breaking out of the container and to facilitate the detection of any tampering with the container while in transit;

b. For DoD contractors indicate on the BL, "Constant Surveillance Service Required." In addition, annotate the BL as indicated in 5-408e.

c. Instruct the carrier to ship packages weighing less than 200 pounds gross in a closed vehicle or a closed portion of the carrier's equipment.

5-410. Use of Couriers, Hand Carriers, and Escorts. Contractors who designate cleared employees as couriers, hand carriers, and escorts shall ensure:

a. They are briefed on their responsibility to safeguard classified information.

b. They possess an identification card or badge which contains the contractor's name and the name and a photograph of the employee.

c. The employee retains classified material in his or her personal possession at all times. Arrangements shall be made in advance of departure for overnight storage at a U.S. Government installation or at a cleared contractor's facility that has appropriate storage capability, if needed.

d. If the classified material is being hand carried to a classified meeting or on a visit, an inventory of the material shall be made prior to departure. A copy of the inventory shall be carried by the employee. On the employee's return to the facility, an inventory shall be made of the material for which the employee was charged.

5-411. Use of Commercial Passenger Aircraft for Transmitting Classified Material. Classified material may be hand carried aboard commercial passenger aircraft by cleared employees with the approval of the FSO.

a. **Routine Processing.** Employees hand carrying classified material will be subject to routine processing by airline security agents. Hand-held packages will normally be screened by x-ray examination. If security personnel are not satisfied with the results of the inspection, and the prospective passenger is requested to open a classified package for visual examination the traveler shall inform the screener that the carry-on items contain U.S. Government classified information and cannot be opened. Under no circumstances may the classified material be opened by the traveler or security personnel.

b. **Special Processing.** When routine processing would subject the classified material to compromise or damage; when visual examination is or may be required to successfully screen a classified package; or when classified material is in specialized containers which due to its size, weight, or other physical characteristics cannot be routinely processed, the contractor shall contact the appropriate air carrier in advance to explain the particular circumstances and obtain instructions on the special screening procedures to be followed.

c. **Authorization Letter.** Contractors shall provide employees with written authorization to hand carry classified material on commercial aircraft. The written authorization shall:

(1) Provide the full name, date of birth, height, weight, and signature of the traveler and state that he or she is authorized to transmit classified material;

(2) Describe the type of identification the traveler will present on request;

(3) Describe the material being hand carried and request that it be exempt from opening;

(4) Identify the points of departure, destination, and known transfer points;

(5) Include the name, telephone number, and signature of the FSO, and the location and telephone number of the CSA.

5-412. Use of Escorts for Classified Shipments. If an escort is necessary to ensure the protection of the classified information being transported, a sufficient number of escorts shall be assigned to each classified shipment to ensure continuous surveillance and control over the shipment while in transit. Specific written instructions and operating procedures shall be furnished escorts prior to shipping and shall include the following:

a. Name and address of persons, including alternates, to whom the classified material is to be delivered;

b. Receipting procedures;

c. Means of transportation and the route to be used;

d. Duties of each escort during movement, during stops en route, and during loading and unloading operations; and

e. Emergency and communication procedures.

5-413. Functions of an Escort. Escorts shall be responsible for the following.

a. Accept custody for the shipment by signing a receipt and release custody of the shipment to the consignee after obtaining a signed receipt.

b. When accompanying a classified shipment in an express or freight car, provide continuous observation of the containers and observe adjacent areas during stops or layovers.

c. When traveling in an escort car accompanying a classified shipment via rail, keep the shipment cars under observation and detrain at stops, when practical and time permits, in order to guard the shipment cars and check the cars or containers locks and seals. The escort car (after arrangements with the railroad) should be pre-positioned immediately behind the car used for the classified shipment to enable the escort to keep the shipment car under observation.

d. Maintain liaison with train crews, other railroad personnel, special police, and law enforcement agencies, as necessary.

e. When escorting classified shipments via motor vehicles, maintain continuous vigilance for the presence of conditions or situations that might threaten the security of the cargo, take such action as circumstances might require to avoid interference with continuous safe passage of the vehicle, check seals and locks at each stop where time permits, and observe vehicles and adjacent areas during stops or layovers.

f. When escorting shipments via aircraft, provide continuous observation of plane and cargo during ground stops and of cargo during loading and unloading operations. The escort shall not board the plane until after the cargo area is secured. Furthermore, the escort should preferably be the first person to depart the plane to observe the opening of the cargo area. Advance arrangements with the airline are required.

g. Notify the consignor by the fastest means available if there is an unforeseen delay en route, an alternate route is used, or an emergency occurs. If appropriate and the security of the shipment is involved, notify the nearest law enforcement official.

Section 5. Disclosure

5-500. General. Contractors shall ensure that classified information is disclosed only to authorized persons.

5-501. Disclosure to Employees. Contractors are authorized to disclose classified information to their cleared employees as necessary for the performance of tasks or services essential to the fulfillment of a classified contract or subcontract.

5-502. Disclosure to Subcontractors. Contractors are authorized to disclose classified information to a cleared subcontractor when access is necessary for the performance of tasks or services essential to the fulfillment of a prime contract or a subcontract.

5-503. Disclosure between Parent and Subsidiaries. Disclosure of classified information between a parent and its subsidiaries, or between subsidiaries, shall be accomplished in the same manner as prescribed in 5-502 for subcontractors.

5-504. Disclosure in an MFO. Disclosure of classified information between cleared facilities of the MFO shall be accomplished in the same manner as prescribed in 5-501 for employees.

5-505. Disclosure to DoD Activities. Contractors are authorized to disclose classified information received or generated under a DoD classified contract to another DoD activity unless specifically prohibited by the DoD activity that has classification jurisdiction over the information.

5-506. Disclosure to Federal Agencies. Contractors shall not disclose classified information received or generated under a contract from one agency to any other Federal agency unless specifically authorized by the agency that has classification jurisdiction over the information.

5-507. Disclosure of Classified Information to Foreign Persons. Contractors shall not disclose classified information to foreign persons unless release of the information is authorized in writing by the Government Agency having classification jurisdiction over the information involved, e.g. the DOE for RD and FRD, the NSA for COMSEC, the DNI for SCI, and all other Executive Branch departments and agencies for classified information under their jurisdiction. The disclosure must also be consistent with applicable U.S. laws and regulations.

5-508. Disclosure of Export Controlled Information to Foreign Persons. Contractors shall not disclose export-controlled information and technology (classified or unclassified) to a foreign person, whether an employee or not, or whether disclosure occurs in the United States or abroad, unless such disclosure is in compliance with applicable U.S. laws and regulations.

5-509. Disclosure to Other Contractors. Contractors shall not disclose classified information to another contractor except in furtherance of a contract, subcontract, or other GCA purpose.

5-510. Disclosure of Classified Information in Connection with Litigation. Contractors shall not disclose classified information to attorneys hired solely to represent the contractor in any civil or criminal case in Federal or state courts unless the disclosure is specifically authorized by the agency that has jurisdiction over the information. Contractors shall not disclose classified information to any Federal or state court except on specific instructions of the agency which has jurisdiction over the information or the attorney representing the United States in the case. (For criminal cases in Federal courts, see paragraph 1-208.)

5-511. Disclosure to the Public. Contractors shall not disclose classified or unclassified information pertaining to a classified contract to the public without prior review and clearance as specified in the Contract Security Classification Specification for the contract or as otherwise specified by the GCA.

a. Requests for approval shall be submitted through the activity specified in the GCA-provided classification guidance for the contract involved. Each request shall indicate the approximate date the contractor intends to release the information for public disclosure and identify the media to be used for the initial release. A copy of each approved request for release shall be retained for a period of one inspection cycle for review by the CSA. All information developed subsequent to the initial approval shall also be cleared by the appropriate office prior to public disclosure.

b. The following information need not be submitted for approval unless specifically prohibited by the GCA:

(1) The fact that a contract has been received, including the subject matter of the contract and/or type

of item in general terms provided the name or description of the subject matter is not classified.

(2) The method or type of contract; such as, bid, negotiated, or letter.

(3) Total dollar amount of the contract unless that information equates to (a) a level of effort in a sensitive research area, or (b) quantities of stocks of certain weapons and equipment that are classified.

(4) Whether the contract will require the hiring or termination of employees.

(5) Other information that from time-to-time may be authorized on a case-by-case basis in a specific agreement with the contractor.

(6) Information previously officially approved for public disclosure.

c. The procedures of this paragraph also apply to information pertaining to classified contracts intended for use in unclassified brochures, promotional sales literature, reports to stockholders, or similar material.

d. Information that has been declassified is not automatically authorized for public disclosure. Contractors shall request approval for public disclosure of "declassified" information in accordance with the procedures of this paragraph.

Section 6. Reproduction

5-600. General. Contractors shall establish a control system to ensure that reproduction of classified material is held to the minimum consistent with contractual and operational requirements. Classified reproduction shall be accomplished by authorized personnel knowledgeable of the procedures. The use of technology that prevents, discourages, or detects the unauthorized reproduction of classified documents is encouraged.

5-601. Limitations

a. TOP SECRET documents may be reproduced as necessary in the preparation of a contract deliverable. Reproduction for any other purpose requires the consent of the GCA.

b. Unless restricted by the GCA, SECRET and CONFIDENTIAL documents may be reproduced as follows:

(1) Performance of a prime contract or a subcontract in furtherance of a prime contract.

(2) Preparation of a solicited or unsolicited bid, quotation, or proposal to a Federal agency or prospective subcontractor.

(3) Preparation of patent applications to be filed in the U.S. Patent Office.

c. Reproduced copies of classified documents shall be subject to the same protection as the original documents.

5-602. Marking Reproductions. All reproductions of classified material shall be conspicuously marked with the same classification markings as the material being reproduced. Copies of classified material shall be reviewed after the reproduction process to ensure that these markings are visible.

5-603. Records. Contractors shall maintain a record of the reproduction of all TOP SECRET material for 2 years.

Section 7. Disposition and Retention

5-700. General

a. Classified information no longer needed shall be processed for appropriate disposition. Classified information approved for destruction shall be destroyed in accordance with this section. The method of destruction must preclude recognition or reconstruction of the classified information or material.

b. Contractors shall establish procedures for review of their classified holdings on a recurring basis to reduce these classified inventories to the minimum necessary for effective and efficient operations. Multiple copies, obsolete material, and classified waste shall be destroyed as soon as practical after it has served its purpose. Any appropriate downgrading and declassification actions shall be taken on a timely basis to reduce the volume and to lower the level of classified material being retained by the contractor.

5-701. Retention of Classified Material. Contractors are authorized to retain classified material received or generated under a contract for a period of 2 years after completion of the contract, provided the GCA does not advise to the contrary. If retention is required beyond the 2-year period, the contractor must request and receive written retention authority from the GCA.

a. Contractors shall identify classified material for retention beyond 2 years as follows:

(1) TOP SECRET material shall be identified in a list of specific documents unless the GCA authorizes identification by subject matter and approximate number of documents.

(2) SECRET and CONFIDENTIAL material may be identified by general subject matter and the approximate number of documents.

b. Contractors shall include a statement of justification for retention based on the following:

(1) The material is necessary for the maintenance of the contractor's essential records.

(2) The material is patentable or proprietary data to which the contractor has title.

(3) The material will assist the contractor in independent research and development efforts.

(4) The material will benefit the U.S. Government in the performance of other prospective or existing agency contracts.

(5) The material will benefit the U.S. Government in the performance of another active contract and will be transferred to that contract (specify contract).

c. If retention beyond 2 years is not authorized, all classified material received or generated in the performance of a classified contract shall be destroyed unless it has been declassified or the GCA has requested that the material be returned.

5-702. Termination of Security Agreement. Notwithstanding the provisions for retention outlined above, in the event that the FCL is to be terminated, the contractor shall return all classified material in its possession to the GCA concerned, or dispose of such material in accordance with instructions from the CSA.

5-703. Disposition of Classified Material Not Received Under a Specific Contract.

a. Contractors shall return or destroy classified material received with a bid, proposal, or quote in accordance with the following schedule:

(1) If a bid, proposal, or quote is not submitted or is withdrawn within 180 days after the opening date of bids, proposals, or quotes.

(2) If a bid, proposal, or quote is not accepted within 180 days after notification that a bid, proposal, or quote has not been accepted.

b. If the classified material was not received under a specific contract, such as material obtained at classified meetings or from a secondary distribution center, within 1 year after receipt.

5-704. Destruction. Contractors shall destroy classified material in their possession as soon as possible after it has served the purpose for which it was released by the government, developed or prepared by the contractor, or retained after completion or termination of the contract.

5-705. Methods of Destruction. Classified material may be destroyed by burning, shredding, pulping, melting, mutilation, chemical decomposition, or pulverizing (for example, hammer mills, choppers, and hybridized disintegration equipment). Pulpers, pulverizers, or shredders may be used only for the destruction of paper products. High wet strength paper, paper mylar, durable-medium paper substitute, or similar water repellent papers are not sufficiently destroyed by pulping; other methods such as disintegration, shredding, or burning shall be used to destroy these types of papers. Residue shall be inspected during each destruction to ensure that classified information cannot be reconstructed. Crosscut shredders currently in use capable of maintaining a shred size not exceeding 1/32 inch in width (with a 1/64 inch tolerance by 1/2 inch in length) may continue to be used. However, any crosscut shredders requiring replacement of the unit and/or rebuilding of the shredder blades assembly must be replaced by a crosscut shredder on the latest NSA Evaluated Products List of High Security Crosscut Shredders. The list may be obtained from the CSA. Classified material in microform; that is, microfilm, microfiche, or similar high data density material; may be destroyed by burning or chemical decomposition, or other methods as approved by the CSA.

a. Public destruction facilities may be used only with the approval of, and under conditions prescribed by, the CSA.

b. Classified material removed from a cleared facility for destruction shall be destroyed on the same day it is removed.

5-706. Witness to Destruction. Classified material shall be destroyed by authorized personnel who have a full understanding of their responsibilities. For destruction of TOP SECRET material, two persons are required. For destruction of SECRET and CONFIDENTIAL material, one person is required.

5-707. Destruction Records. Destruction records are required for TOP SECRET material. The records shall indicate the date of destruction, identify the material destroyed, and be signed by the individuals designated to destroy and witness the destruction. Destruction officials shall be required to know, through their personal knowledge, that such material was destroyed. At the contractor's discretion, the destruction information required may be combined with other required control records. Destruction records shall be maintained by the contractor for 2 years.

5-708. Classified Waste. Classified waste shall be destroyed as soon as practical. This applies to all waste material containing classified information. Pending destruction, classified waste shall be safeguarded as required for the level of classified material involved. Receptacles utilized to accumulate classified waste shall be clearly identified as containing classified material.

Section 8. Construction Requirements

5-800. General. This section describes the construction requirements for closed areas and vaults. Construction shall conform to the requirements of this section or, with CSA approval, to the standards of Intelligence Community (IC) Directive 705, "Sensitive Compartmented Information Facilities (SCIFs) (reference (n)).

5-801. Construction Requirements for Closed Areas. This paragraph specifies the minimum safeguards and standards required for the construction of closed areas that are approved for use for safeguarding classified material. These criteria and standards apply to all new construction and reconstruction, alterations, modifications, and repairs of existing areas. They will also be used for evaluating the adequacy of existing areas.

a. **Hardware.** Only heavy-gauge hardware shall be used in construction. Hardware accessible from outside the area shall be peened, pinned, brazed, or spot welded to preclude removal.

b. **Walls.** Construction may be of material offering resistance to, and evidence of, unauthorized entry into the area. If insert-type panels are used, a method shall be devised to prevent the removal of such panels without leaving visual evidence of tampering. If visual access is a factor, area barrier walls up to a height of 8 feet shall be of opaque or translucent construction.

c. **Windows.** Windows that can be opened and that are less than 18 feet from an access point (for example, another window outside the area, roof, ledge, or door) shall be fitted with 1/2-inch bars (separated by no more than 6 inches), plus crossbars to prevent spreading, 18-gauge expanded metal or wire mesh securely fastened on the inside. When visual access of classified information is a factor, the windows shall be covered by any practical method, such as drapes, blinds, or paint covering the inside of the glass. During nonworking hours, the windows shall be closed and securely fastened to preclude surreptitious entry.

d. **Doors.** Doors shall be constructed of material offering resistance to and detection of unauthorized entry. When windows, louvers, baffle plates, or similar openings are used, they shall be secured with 18-gauge expanded metal or with wire mesh securely fastened on the inside. If visual access is a factor, the windows shall be covered. When doors are used in

pairs, an astragal (overlapping molding) shall be installed where the doors meet.

e. **Door Locking Devices.** Entrance doors shall be secured with either an approved built-in combination lock, an approved combination padlock, or with an approved key-operated padlock. Other doors shall be secured from the inside with a panic bolt (for example, actuated by a panic bar); a dead bolt; a rigid wood or metal bar (which shall preclude "springing") which extends across the width of the door and is held in position by solid clamps, preferably on the door casing; or by other means approved by the CSA consistent with relevant fire and safety codes.

f. **Ceilings.** Ceilings shall be constructed of material offering resistance to and detection of unauthorized entry. Wire mesh or other non-opaque material offering similar resistance to, and evidence of, unauthorized entry into the area may be used if visual access to classified material is not a factor.

g. **Ceilings (Unusual Cases).** When wall barriers do not extend to the true ceiling and a false ceiling is created, the false ceiling must be reinforced with wire mesh or 18-gauge expanded metal to serve as the true ceiling. When wire mesh or expanded metal is used, it must overlap the adjoining walls and be secured in a manner that precludes removal without leaving evidence of tampering. When wall barriers of an area do extend to the true ceiling and a false ceiling is added, there is no necessity for reinforcing the false ceiling. When there is a valid justification for not erecting a solid ceiling as part of the area, such as the use of overhead cranes for the movement of bulky equipment within the area, the contractor shall ensure that surreptitious entry cannot be obtained by entering the area over the top of the barrier walls.

h. **Miscellaneous Openings.** All vents, ducts and similar openings into closed areas that measure in excess of 96 square inches and over 6 inches in their smallest dimension must be protected with either ½-inch diameter steel bars with a maximum space of 6 inches between the bars; grills consisting of 18-gauge expanded metal, wire mesh; or an equivalent gauge commercial metal duct barrier. The barriers must be secured to preclude removal from outside the area, and the method of installation must ensure that classified material cannot be removed through the openings with the aid of any type of instrument. A barrier will not be required if an approved IDS provides protection of the opening.

5-802. Construction Required for Vaults. This paragraph specifies the minimum standards required for the construction of vaults approved for use as storage facilities for classified material. These standards apply to all new construction and reconstruction, alterations, modifications, and repairs of existing vaults. They will also be used for evaluating the adequacy of existing vaults. In addition to the requirements given below, the wall, floor, and roof construction shall be in accordance with nationally recognized standards of structural practice. For the vaults described below, the concrete shall be poured in place and will have a compressive strength of 2,500 pounds per square inch.

a. **Floor.** The floor must be a monolithic concrete construction of the thickness of adjacent concrete floor construction, but not less than 4 inches thick.

b. **Walls.** Walls must be not less than 8-inch-thick hollow clay tile (vertical cell double shells) or concrete blocks (thick shells). Monolithic steel-reinforced concrete walls at least 4 inches thick may also be used. Where hollow clay tiles are used and such masonry units are flush, or in contact with, facility exterior walls, they shall be filled with concrete and steel-reinforced bars. Walls are to extend to the underside of the roof or ceiling above.

c. **Roof/Ceiling.** The roof or ceiling must be a monolithic reinforced concrete slab of a thickness to be determined by structural requirements.

d. **Vault Door and Frame Unit.** A GSA-approved vault door and frame unit shall be used.

e. **Miscellaneous Openings.** Omission of all miscellaneous openings is desirable, but not mandatory. Openings of such size and shape as to permit unauthorized entry, (normally in excess of 96 square inches in area and over 6 inches in its smallest dimension) and openings for ducts, pipes, registers, sewers and tunnels shall be equipped with man-safe barriers such as wire mesh, 18-gauge expanded metal, or rigid metal bars of at least 1/2 inch in diameter extending across their width with a maximum space of 6 inches between the bars. The rigid metal bars shall be securely fastened at both ends to preclude removal and, if the bars exceed 18 inches in length, shall have crossbars to prevent spreading. Where wire mesh, expanded metal, or rigid metal bars are used, care shall be exercised to ensure that classified material within the vault cannot be removed with the aid of any type of instrument. Pipes and conduits entering the vault shall enter through walls that are not common to the vault and the structure housing the vault. Preferably such pipes and conduits should be installed when the vault is constructed. If this is not practical, they shall be carried through snug-fitting pipe sleeves cast in the concrete. After installation, the annular space between the sleeve and the pipe or conduit shall be caulked solid with lead, wood, waterproof (silicone) caulking, or similar material, which will give evidence of surreptitious removal.

Section 9. Intrusion Detection Systems

5-900. General. This section specifies the minimum standards for an approved IDS when supplemental protection is required for TOP SECRET and SECRET material. The IDS shall be connected to, and monitored by, a central monitoring station. Alarm system installation shall conform to the requirements of this section or to the standards set forth in reference (n). The CSA will approve contingency protection procedures in the event of IDS malfunction.

5-901. CSA Approval

a. CSA approval is required before installing an IDS. Approval of a new IDS shall be based on the criteria of reference (n) or UL Standard 2050, reference (o), as determined by the CSA.

b. The UL listed Alarm Service Company (ASC) is responsible for completing the Alarm System Description Form.

5-902. Central Monitoring Station

a. The central monitoring station may be located at a UL-listed: (1) Government Contractor Monitoring Station (GCMS), formerly called a proprietary central station; (2) cleared commercial central station; (3) cleared protective signal service station (e.g., fire alarm monitor); or (4) cleared residential monitoring station. For the purpose of monitoring alarms, all provide an equivalent level of monitoring service.

b. SECRET-cleared central station employees shall be in attendance at the alarm monitoring station in sufficient number to monitor each alarmed area within the cleared contractor facility.

c. The central monitoring station shall be required to indicate whether or not the system is in working order and to indicate tampering with any element of the system. Necessary repairs shall be made as soon as practical. Until repairs are completed, periodic patrols shall be conducted during non-working hours, unless a SECRET cleared employee is stationed at the alarmed site.

d. When an IDS is used, it shall be activated immediately at the close of business at the alarmed area or container. This may require that the last person who departs the controlled area or checks the security container notify the central monitoring station to set the alarm. A record shall be maintained to identify the person responsible for setting and deactivating the IDS. Each failure to activate or deactivate shall be reported to the FSO. Such records shall be maintained for 30 days.

e. Records shall be maintained for 90 days indicating time of receipt of alarm, name(s) of security force personnel responding, time dispatched to facility/area, time security force personnel arrived, nature of alarm, and what follow-up actions were accomplished.

5-903. Investigative Response to Alarms. The primary purpose of any alarm response team is to ascertain if intrusion has occurred and if possible assist in the apprehension of the individuals involved. If an alarm activation resets in a reasonable amount of time and no damage to the area or container is visible, then entrance into the area or container is not required. Therefore, the initial response team may consist of uncleared personnel. If the alarm activation does not reset and damage is observed, then a cleared response team must be dispatched. The initial uncleared response team must stay on station until relieved by the cleared response team. If a cleared response team does not arrive within one hour, then a report to the CSA must be made by the close of the next business day.

a. The following resources may be used to investigate alarms: proprietary security force personnel, central station guards, or a subcontracted guard service.

(1) For a GCMS, trained proprietary or subcontractor security force personnel, cleared to the SECRET level and sufficient in number to be dispatched immediately to investigate each alarm, shall be available at all times when the IDS is in operation.

(2) For a commercial central station, protective signaling service station, or residential monitoring station, there shall be a sufficient number of trained guards available to respond to alarms. Guards shall be cleared only if they have the ability and responsibility to access the area or container(s) housing classified material; i.e., keys to the facility have been provided or the personnel are authorized to enter the building or check the container or area that contains classified material.

(3) Uncleared guards dispatched by a commercial central station, protective signaling service station, or residential monitoring station in response to an alarm shall remain on the premises until a

designated, cleared representative of the facility arrives, or for a period of not less than 1 hour, whichever comes first. If a cleared representative of the facility does not arrive within 1 hour following the arrival of the guard, the central control station must provide the CSA with a report of the incident that includes the name of the subscriber facility, the date and time of the alarm, and the name of the subscriber's representative who was contacted to respond. A report shall be submitted to the CSA within 24 hours of the next working day.

(4) Subcontracted guards must be under a classified contract with either the installing alarm company or the cleared facility.

b. The response time shall not exceed 15 minutes. When environmental factors (e.g., traffic, distance) legitimately prevent a 15-minute response time, the CSA may authorize up to a 30-minute response time. The CSA approval shall be documented on the UL Alarm System Description Form and the specified response time shall be noted on the alarm certificate. The UL standard for response within the time limits is 80%. That is the minimum allowable on-time response rate and anything less than 80% is unacceptable. However, in all cases, a guard or cleared employee must arrive at the alarmed premises.

5-904. Installation. The IDS at the facility, area or container shall be installed by a UL listed ASC or by a company approved by the CSA. When connected to a commercial central station, GCMS protective signaling service or residential monitoring station, the service provided shall include line security (i.e., the connecting lines are electronically supervised to detect evidence of tampering or malfunction), the extent of protection for a container shall be "Complete," and for an alarmed area shall be "Extent 3" as described in the reference (o) installation guide. CSA authorization on the Alarm System Description Form is required in the following circumstances:

a. Line security is not available. Installation will require two independent means of transmission of the alarm signal from the alarmed area to the monitoring station.

b. Alarm installation provides Extent 5 Protection. Reference (o) allows for Extent 5 based on patrolling guards and CSA approval of security-in-depth.

c. Law enforcement personnel are the primary alarm response. The contractor must obtain written

assurance from the police department regarding the ability to respond to alarms.

d. Alarm signal transmission is over computer controlled data-networks (internet, intranet, etc.). The CSA will provide specific acceptance criteria (e.g., encryption requirements, etc.) for alarms monitored over data networks.

e. Alarm investigator response time exceeds 15 minutes.

5-905. Certification of Compliance. Evidence of compliance with the requirements of this section will consist of a valid (current) UL Certificate for the appropriate category of service. This certificate will have been issued to the protected facility by UL, through the alarm installing company. The certificate serves as evidence that the alarm installing company: (a) is listed as furnishing security systems of the category indicated; (b) is authorized to issue the certificate of installation as representation that the equipment is in compliance with requirements established by UL for the class; and (c) is subject to the UL field countercheck program whereby periodic inspections are made of representative alarm installations by UL personnel to verify the correctness of certification practices.

5-906. Exceptional Cases

a. If the requirements set forth above cannot be met, the contractor may request CSA approval for an alarm system meeting one of the conditions listed below. CSA approval will be documented on the Alarm System Description Form.

(1) Monitored by a central control station but responded to by a local (municipal, county, state) law enforcement organization.

(2) Connected by direct wire to alarm receiving equipment located in a local (municipal, county, state) police station or public emergency service dispatch center. This alarm system is activated and deactivated by employees of the contractor, but the alarm is monitored and responded to by personnel of the monitoring police or emergency service dispatch organization. Personnel monitoring alarm signals at police stations or dispatch centers do not require PCLs. Police department response systems may be requested only when: (a) the contractor facility is located in an area where central control station services are not available with line security and/or proprietary security force personnel, or a contractually-dispatched response to an alarm signal cannot be achieved within the time

limits required by the CSA, and, (b) it is impractical for the contractor to establish a GCMS or proprietary guard force at that location. Nonetheless, installation of these systems must use UL-listed equipment and be accomplished by an ASC Service Center listed by UL for any of the following categories:

    1. Defense (National) Industrial Security Systems

    2. Proprietary Alarm Systems

    3. Central Station Burglar Alarm Systems

    4. Police - Station - Connected Burglar Alarm Systems

b. An installation proposal, explaining how the system would operate, shall be submitted to the CSA. The proposal must include sufficient justification for the granting of an exception and the full name and address of the police department that will monitor the system and provide the required response. The name and address of the UL listed company that will install the system, and inspect, maintain, and repair the equipment, shall also be furnished.

c. The contractor shall require a 15-minute response time from the police department. Arrangements shall be made with the police to immediately notify a contractor representative on receipt of the alarm. The contractor representative is required to go immediately to the facility to investigate the alarm and to take appropriate measures to secure the classified material.

d. In exceptional cases where central station monitoring service is available, but no proprietary security force, central station, or subcontracted guard response is available, and where the police department does not agree to respond to alarms, and no other manner of investigative response is available, the CSA may approve cleared employees as the sole means of response.

CHAPTER 6
Visits and Meetings

Section 1. Visits

6-100. General. This section applies when, for a lawful and authorized U.S. Government purpose, it is anticipated that classified information will be disclosed during a visit to a cleared contractor or to a Federal facility.

6-101. Classified Visits. The number of classified visits shall be held to a minimum. The contractor must determine that the visit is necessary and that the purpose of the visit cannot be achieved without access to, or disclosure of, classified information. Contractors shall establish procedures to ensure positive identification of visitors, appropriate PCL, and need-to-know prior to the disclosure of any classified information. Contractors shall establish procedures to ensure that visitors are only afforded access to classified information consistent with the purpose of the visit.

6-102. Need-to-Know Determination. The responsibility for determining need-to-know in connection with a classified visit rests with the individual who will disclose classified information during the visit. Need-to-know is generally based on a contractual relationship between the contractors. In other circumstances, disclosure of the information will be based on an assessment that the receiving contractor has a bona fide need to access the information in furtherance of a GCA purpose.

6-103. Visits by Government Representatives. Representatives of the Federal Government, when acting in their official capacities as inspectors, investigators, or auditors, may visit a contractor's facility, provided these representatives present appropriate government credentials upon arrival.

6-104. Visit Authorization

a. If a visit requires access to classified information, the host contractor shall verify the visitor's PCL level. Verification of a visitor's PCL may be accomplished by a review of a CSA-designated database that contains the information or by a visit authorization letter (VAL) provided by the visitor's employer.

b. If a CSA-designated database is not available and a VAL is required, contractors shall include the following information in all VALs.

(1). Contractor's name, address, and telephone number, assigned Commercial and Government Entity (CAGE) code, if applicable, and certification of the level of the facility security clearance;

(2). Name, date and place of birth, and citizenship of the employee intending to visit;

(3). Certification of the proposed visitor's PCL and any special access authorizations required for the visit;

(4). Name of person(s) to be visited;

(5). Purpose and sufficient justification for the visit to allow for a determination of the necessity of the visit; and

(6). Date or period during which the VAL is to be valid.

6-105. Long-Term Visitors

a. When government employees or employees of one contractor are temporarily stationed at another contractor's facility, the security procedures of the host contractor will govern.

b. Government personnel assigned to or visiting a contractor facility and engaged in oversight of an acquisition program shall retain control of their work product. Classified work products of government employees shall be handled in accordance with this Manual. Contractor procedures shall not require government employees to relinquish control of their work products, whether classified or not, to a contractor.

c. Contractor employees at government installations shall follow the security requirements of the host. However, this does not relieve the contractor from security oversight of their employees who are long-term visitors at government installations.

Section 2. Meetings

6-200. General. This section applies to a conference, seminar, symposium, exhibit, convention, training course, or other such gathering during which classified information is disclosed, hereafter called a "meeting."

6-201. Government Sponsorship of Meetings. Disclosure of classified information to large diverse audiences such as conferences increases security risks. However, classified disclosure at such meetings which serve a government purpose and at which adequate security measures have been provided in advance may be conducted by a cleared contractor provided the meeting is authorized by a government agency that has agreed to assume security jurisdiction. The government agency must approve security arrangements, announcements, attendees, and the location of the meeting. The government agency may delegate certain responsibilities to a cleared contractor for the security arrangements and other actions necessary for the meeting under the general supervision of the government agency.

a. **Requests for Authorization.** Contractors desiring to conduct meetings requiring sponsorship shall submit their requests to the Government Agency having principal interest in the subject matter of each meeting. The request for authorization shall include the following information:

(1) An explanation of the government purpose to be served by disclosing classified information at the meeting and why the use of conventional channels for release of the information will not advance those interests.

(2) The subject of the meeting and scope of classified topics, to include the classification level, to be disclosed at the meeting.

(3) The expected dates and location of the meeting.

(4) The general content of the proposed announcement and/or invitation to be sent to prospective attendees or participants.

(5) The identity of any other non-government organization involved and a full description of the type of support it will provide.

(6) A list of any foreign representatives (including their nationality, name, organizational affiliation) whose attendance at the meeting is proposed.

(7) A description of the security arrangements necessary for the meeting to comply with the requirements of this Manual.

b. **Location of Meetings.** Classified sessions shall be held only at a Federal Government installation or a cleared contractor facility where adequate physical security and procedural controls have been approved. The authorizing government agency is responsible for evaluating and approving the location proposed for the meeting.

c. **Security Arrangements for Meetings.** The contractor shall develop the security measures and procedures to be used and obtain the authorizing agency's approval. The security arrangements must provide for the following:

(1) **Announcements.** Approval of the authorizing agency shall be obtained for all announcements of the meeting. Announcements shall be unclassified and shall be limited to a general description of topics expected to be presented, names of speakers, and administrative instructions for requesting invitations or participation. Classified presentations shall not be solicited in the announcement. When the meeting has been approved, announcements may only state that the government agency has authorized the conduct of classified sessions and will provide necessary security assistance. The announcement shall further specify that security clearances and justification to attend classified sessions are to be forwarded to the authorizing agency or its designee. Invitations to foreign persons shall be sent by the authorizing government agency.

(2) **Clearance and Need-to-know.** All persons in attendance at classified sessions shall possess the requisite clearance and need-to-know for the information to be disclosed. Need-to-know shall be determined by the authorizing agency or its designee based on the justification provided. Attendance shall be authorized only to those persons whose security clearance and justification for attendance have been verified by the security officer of the organization represented. The names of all authorized attendees or participants must appear on an

access list with entry permitted to the classified session only after verification of the attendee's identity based on presentation of official photographic identification such as a passport, contractor or U.S. Government identification card.

(3) **Presentations.** Classified information must be authorized for disclosure in advance by the government agency having jurisdiction over the information to be presented. Individuals making presentations at meetings shall provide sufficient classification guidance to enable attendees to identify what information is classified and the level of classification. Classified presentations shall be delivered orally and/or visually. Copies of classified presentations or slides, etc., shall not be distributed at the classified meeting, and any classified notes or electronic recordings of classified presentations shall be classified, safeguarded, and transmitted as required by this Manual.

(4) **Physical Security.** The physical security measures for the classified sessions shall provide for control of, access to, and dissemination of, the classified information to be presented and shall provide for secure storage capability, if necessary.

6-202. Disclosure Authority at Meetings. A contractor desiring to disclose classified information at a meeting shall:

a. Obtain prior written authorization for each proposed disclosure of classified information from the government agency having jurisdiction over the information involved.

b. Furnish a copy of the disclosure authorization to the government agency sponsoring the meeting.

c. Associations are not responsible for ensuring that classified presentations and papers of other organizations have been approved for disclosure. Authority to disclose classified information at meetings, whether disclosure is by officials of industry or government, must be granted by the government agency or activity that has classification jurisdiction over the information to be disclosed. Each contractor that desires to disclose classified information at a meeting is responsible for requesting and obtaining disclosure approvals.

6-203. Requests to Attend Classified Meetings. Before a contractor employee can attend a classified meeting, the contractor shall provide justification why the employee requires access to the classified information, cite the classified contract or GCA program/project involved, and forward the information to the authorizing government agency.

CHAPTER 7
Subcontracting

Section 1. Prime Contractor Responsibilities

7-100. General. This Chapter outlines the requirements and responsibilities of a prime contractor when disclosing classified information to a subcontractor.

7-101. Responsibilities. Before a prime contractor may release or disclose classified information to a subcontractor, or cause classified information to be generated by a subcontractor, the following actions are required:

a. Determine the security requirements of the subcontract.

(1) Access to classified information will be required. This is a "classified contract" within the meaning of this Manual. A "security requirements clause" and a Contract Security Classification Specification shall be incorporated in the solicitation and in the subcontract (see the "security requirements clause" in the prime contract). The subcontractor must possess an appropriate FCL and safeguarding capability if possession of classified information will be required.

(a) If access will not be required in the pre-award phase, prospective subcontractors are not required to possess an FCL to receive or bid on the solicitation.

(b) If access will be required during the pre-award phase, all prospective subcontractors must possess the appropriate FCL and have safeguarding capability.

(2) Access to classified information will not be required. This is not a classified contract within the meaning of this Manual. If the prime contract contains requirements for release or disclosure of certain information even though not classified, such as sensitive but unclassified information, the requirements shall be incorporated in the solicitation and the subcontract.

b. Determine clearance status of prospective subcontractors.

(1) All prospective subcontractors have appropriate clearance. This determination can be made if there is an existing contractual relationship between the parties involving classified information of the same or higher category, by accessing the CSA-designated database, or by contacting the CSA.

(2) If a prospective subcontractor does not have the appropriate FCL or safeguarding capability, the prime contractor shall request the CSA of the subcontractor to initiate the necessary action. Requests shall include, as a minimum, the full name, address and contact information for the requester; the full name, address, and contact information for a contact at the facility to be processed for an FCL; the level of clearance and/or safeguarding capability required; and full justification for the request. Requests for safeguarding capability shall include a description, quantity, end-item, and classification of the information related to the proposed subcontract. Other factors necessary to help the CSA determine if the prospective subcontractor meets the requirements of this Manual shall be identified, such as any special access requirements.

c. Requesting contractors shall allow sufficient lead time in connection with the award of a classified subcontract to enable an uncleared bidder to be processed for the necessary FCL. When the FCL cannot be granted in sufficient time to qualify the prospective subcontractor for participation in the current procurement action, the CSA will continue the FCL processing action to qualify the prospective subcontractor for future contract consideration provided:

(1) The delay in processing the FCL was not caused by a lack of cooperation on the part of the prospective subcontractor;

(2) Future classified negotiations may occur within 12 months; and

(3) There is reasonable likelihood the subcontractor may be awarded a classified subcontract.

7-102. Security Classification Guidance. Prime contractors shall ensure that a Contract Security Classification Specification is incorporated in each classified subcontract. When preparing classification guidance for a subcontract, the prime contractor may extract pertinent information from the Contract Security Classification Specification issued with the prime contract; from security classification guides issued with the prime contract; or from any security guides that provide guidance for the classified information furnished to, or that will be generated by, the subcontractor. The Contract Security Classification Specification prepared by the prime contractor shall be certified by a designated official of the contractor. In the absence of exceptional circumstances, the classification specification shall not contain any classified information. If classified supplements are required as part of the Contract Security Classification Specification, they shall be identified and forwarded to the subcontractor by separate correspondence.

a. An original Contract Security Classification Specification shall be included with each RFQ, RFP, IFB, or other solicitation to ensure that the prospective subcontractor is aware of the security requirements of the subcontract and can plan accordingly. An original Contract Security Classification Specification shall also be included in the subcontract awarded to the successful bidder.

b. A revised Contract Security Classification Specification shall be issued as necessary during the lifetime of the subcontract when the security requirements change.

c. Requests for public release by a subcontractor shall be forwarded through the prime contractor to the GCA.

7-103. Responsibilities (Completion of the Subcontract). Upon completion of the subcontract, the subcontractor may retain classified material received or generated under the subcontract for a 2-year period, provided the prime contractor or GCA does not advise to the contrary. If retention is required beyond the 2-year period, the subcontractor must request written retention authority through the prime contractor to the GCA. If retention authority is approved by the GCA, the prime contractor will issue a final Contract Security Classification Specification, annotated to provide the retention period and final disposition instructions.

7-104. Notification of Unsatisfactory Conditions. The prime contractor shall be notified if the CSA discovers unsatisfactory security conditions in a subcontractor's facility. When so notified, the prime contractor shall follow the instructions received relative to what action, if any, should be taken in order to safeguard classified material relating to the subcontract.

CHAPTER 8
IS Security

Section 1. Responsibilities and Duties

8-100. General

a. Contractor ISs that are used to capture, create, store, process or distribute classified information must be properly managed to protect against unauthorized disclosure of classified information. Protection concerning loss of availability or integrity of the information on the system must be established separately by contract. ISs security will use a risk-based approach, including a baseline set of management, operational, and technical controls.

b. Protection requires a balanced approach including ISs security features to include but not limited to, administrative, operational, physical, computer, communications, and personnel controls. Protective measures commensurate with the classification of the information, the threat, and the operational requirements associated with the environment of the ISs are required.

c. Banners will be included on all classified ISs to notify users they are subject to monitoring and that such monitoring could be used against them in a criminal, security, or administrative proceeding.

d. The contractor will implement protection measures in accordance with guidance issued by the CSA, including tools or capabilities required by the CSA to monitor user activity on classified ISs in order to detect activity indicative of insider threat behavior. The guidance the CSA issues will be based on requirements for Federal systems, as established by section 3541, et seq. of title 44, U.S.C., also known as the "Federal Information Security Management Act" (reference (ai)) and defined in National Institute of Standards and Technology Special Publication (NIST) 800-37 (reference (aj)), Committee on National Security Systems (CNSS) Directive 504 (reference (ak)), and other applicable CNSS publications (e.g., NIST Special Publication 800-53 (reference (al)) and CNNSI No. 1253 (reference (am)). The CSA may provide profiles containing security controls appropriate for specific types of systems, configurations, and environments.

e. The requirements outlined in the following sections apply to all ISs processing classified information. Additional requirements for high-risk systems and data are covered in Appendix D of this Manual.

8-101. ISs Security Program. The contractor will maintain an ISs security program that incorporates a risk-based set of management, operational and technical controls, consistent with guidelines established by the CSA. The ISs security program must include, at a minimum, the following elements:

a. Policies and procedures that reduce information security risks to an acceptable level and address information security throughout the IS life cycle.

b. Plans for providing adequate information security for data resident in the IS or on the networks, facilities, or groups of ISs, as appropriate.

c. In addition to the training requirements outlined in paragraphs 3-107 and 3-108 of chapter 3 of this Manual, all IS authorized users will receive training on the security risks associated with their user activities and responsibilities under the NISP. The contractor will determine the appropriate content of the security training taking into consideration, assigned roles and responsibilities, specific security requirements, and the ISs to which personnel are authorized access.

d. Testing and evaluation of information security policies, procedures, practices, and security control implementation no less than annually to reflect a continuous monitoring approach of IS related risk assumptions and security control effectiveness.

e. A process for planning, implementing, evaluating, and documenting remedial actions to address any deficiencies in the information security policies, procedures, and practices.

f. Procedures for detecting, reporting, and responding to security incidents and events.

g. Plans and procedures for ISs continuity of operations when required by contract.

h. A self-inspection program in accordance with paragraph 1-207b of chapter 1 of this Manual.

8-102. System Security Plan (SSP). The contractor will document ISs protections in the SSP. The SSP provides a summary of the security requirements for the ISs and describes the security controls in place. The SSP may reference other key security-related documents for the ISs, e.g., a risk assessment, plan of action and milestones, authorization decision letter, contingency plan, configuration management plan, security configuration checklist, and system interconnection agreement, as appropriate.

8-103. Contractor Responsibilities. The contractor will certify to the CSA that the ISs to be used for processing classified information includes an ISs security program that addresses the management, operational, and technical controls in accordance with CSA-provided guidelines. Contractors that are, or will be, processing classified information on an IS must appoint an employee to serve as the ISs Security Manager (ISSM). It is the responsibility of the contractor to assure that the ISSM is adequately trained and possesses technical . competence commensurate with the complexity of the contractor's ISs.

a. The ISSM will:

(1) Oversee the development, implementation, and evaluation of the contractor's ISs program, including insider threat awareness, for facility management, ISs personnel, users, and others, as appropriate. The ISSM must coordinate with the contractor's FSO and the contractor's Insider Threat Program Senior Official to ensure insider threat awareness is addressed within the contractor's ISs program.

(2) Possess sufficient experience, command adequate resources, and be organizationally aligned to ensure prompt support and successful execution of a robust ISs security program.

(3) Develop, document, and monitor compliance with and reporting of the contractor facility's ISs security program in accordance with CSA-provided guidelines for management, operational, and technical controls.

(4) Verify self-inspections are conducted on the contractor's ISs and corrective actions are taken for all identified findings and vulnerabilities.

(5) Certify to the CSA, in writing, each SSP has been implemented; the specified security controls are in place and properly tested; and the IS continues to function as described in the SSP.

(6) Brief users on their responsibilities with regard to ISs security and verify contractor personnel are trained on the ISs prescribed security restrictions and safeguards before they are allowed to access a system.

b. The ISSM may assign an IS Security Officer (ISSO). If assigned, the ISSO will:

(1) Verify the implementation of delegated aspects of the contractor's ISs Security Program from the ISSM and security measures, in accordance with CSA and contractor procedures.

(2) Conduct self-inspections and provide corrective actions to the ISSM.

c. All IS users will:

(1) Comply with the ISs security program requirements as part of their responsibilities for the protection of ISs and classified information.

(2) Be accountable for their actions on an IS.

(3) Not share any authentication mechanisms (including passwords) issued for the control of their access to an IS.

(4) Protect authentication mechanisms at the highest classification level and most restrictive classification category of information to which the mechanisms permit access.

(5) Be subject to monitoring of their activity on any classified network and the results of such monitoring could be used against them in a criminal, security, or administrative proceeding.

Section 2. *Assessment and Authorization*

8-200. Overview. Assessment and authorization of classified networks and ISs is integral to managing information security-related risks. Execution of these tasks helps to ensure security capabilities provided by the selected security controls are implemented, tested, validated, and approved by the authorizing official (AO), designated by the applicable CSA, with a degree of assurance appropriate for their information protection needs.

8-201. Assessment. Security control assessment is a combined effort by the contractor and the CSA. The contractor will review, certify, and attest to the CSA that all systems have the appropriate protection measures in place. The CSA must receive the most complete, accurate, and trustworthy information to make timely, credible, and risk assessment based decisions on whether to authorize ISs operation.

8-202. Authorization. The AO, on behalf of the U.S. Government, will render an operational authorization decision based on the results of security assessment activities and the implementation of the CSA-provided set of security controls. All ISs must be authorized before processing classified information. The AO may choose to eliminate the authorization termination date (ATD) if the contractor's continuous monitoring program is sufficiently robust to provide the AO with needed information with regard to the security state of the ISs and the ongoing effectiveness of security controls in accordance with reference (al) and the Office of Management and Budget Memorandum M-14-03 (reference (an)) or their successors.

a. **Interim Authorization to Operate (IATO).** The AO may grant interim authorization (temporary authority) for an initial period up to 180 days with an option for the AO to extend the interim approval for an additional 180 days. The contractor will have the CSA-approved protection measures in place and functioning during the period of the IATO.

b. **ATO.** The AO may grant an authorization to operate (ATO) following validation of the CSA-approved protection measures conducted during the IATO period, or may grant an ATO without an IATO period.

c. **Security-Relevant Changes.** All modifications to security-relevant resources of an authorized IS (including software, firmware, hardware, or interfaces and interconnections to networks) must be approved in accordance with CSA-provided guidelines before implementation. The CSA will review all security-relevant changes based on provisions of the system configuration management program and CSA guidelines. The contractor will notify the CSA of all changes that deviate from the requirements of the approved SSP. The CSA will then notify the contractor if system reauthorization is required. During the reauthorization process, the CSA may grant an IATO.

(1) Examples of security-relevant changes to an IS that should be reviewed for possible reauthorization include, but are not limited to:

(a) Installation of a new or upgraded operating system, middleware component, or application;

(b) Modifications to networks, nodes, system ports, protocols, or services;

(c) Installation of a new or upgraded hardware platform or firmware component; or

(d) Modifications to cryptographic modules or services.

(2) Changes in laws, directives, policies, or regulations, while not always directly related to the IS, can potentially affect the security of the system and trigger a reauthorization action.

(3) Applying security patches and performing other maintenance actions that do not affect the protection features of the IS, as previously validated by the CSA, are not considered security relevant changes and therefore do not require the reauthorization of an IS.

d. **Re-evaluation of an Authorization.** Each IS will be reevaluated for authorization every 3 years, or at shorter intervals if required by the CSA. The reevaluation of an authorization by a CSA involves input from the ISSM that the conditions under which the original authorization was granted still apply. CSA-provided guidance will include procedures and record-keeping requirements for reevaluation of an authorization as follows:

(1) The IS has no ATD or no security relevant changes.

(2) The IS has an ATD, or has security relevant changes.

e. Withdrawal of Authorization. The CSA will evaluate the risks and consider withdrawal of authorization if the management, operational or technical protection measures approved for the system do not remain effective, or if classified information is placed at risk. The CSA may withdraw authorization at any time based on those considerations. The contractor will sanitize or destroy classified media via approved government procedures when the IS is no longer required to process classified information unless retention has been authorized in accordance with a final contract security classification specification. The method of sanitization or destruction of classified media must be accomplished using CSA guidance before action is taken. Audit logs will be retained for 12 months or until the next inspection.

f. Invalidation of an Authorization. The contractor will notify the applicable CSA personnel (e.g., the AO), whenever detrimental, security-relevant changes occur to any of the following: the required protection level, the operational environment, the interconnections, or as specified in CSA guidelines. If the CSA determines classified information is at risk, the CSA will notify the contractor and the authorization of the IS will become invalid immediately. If the contractor determines classified information on the IS is at risk, the contractor will cease processing classified information on the affected IS and notify the CSA immediately.

Section 3. Security Controls

8-300. Security Controls. This section describes the minimum parameters for management, operational, and technical controls that contractors are required to implement. Additional security controls may be provided by the CSA to establish the baseline security control set required for each IS processing classified information.

8-301. Management Controls. Contractors will apply the following control measures:

   a. **System and Services Acquisition**.

     (1) Allocate sufficient resources to adequately protect ISs.

     (2) Employ system development cycle processes that address information security considerations.

     (3) Employ software usage and installation restrictions.

   b. **Planning**. Contractors will develop, document, maintain, and implement security plans for ISs that describe the security controls in place or planned for the ISs and the rules of behavior for individuals accessing the ISs.

   c. **Security Control Assessments**. As part of the assessment and self-inspection processes, the contractor will:

     (1) Assess the ISs security controls to determine if they are effective.

     (2) Develop and implement plans of action designed to correct deficiencies and reduce or eliminate vulnerabilities.

     (3) Monitor ISs security controls on an ongoing basis to ensure continued effectiveness.

   d. **Program Management**. The contractor will develop and implement an organization-wide information security program that supports the protection of classified information and ISs that process classified information that support the operations and assets of the contractor.

   e. **Risk Assessment**. The contractor will:

     (1) Categorize the potential impact level for confidentiality based on the classification level of the system (CONFIDENTIAL = Low; SECRET = Moderate; TOP SECRET = High).

     (2) When required by contract, protect against the loss of availability or integrity, add the confidentiality impact level with the appropriate impact levels for integrity and availability to determine the security control baseline (e.g., Moderate, Low, Low). Otherwise, when the loss of availability and integrity is not required by contract, the security control baseline will be Low, Low.

     (3) Document the security categorization results (including supporting rationale) in the systems security plan.

     (4) Monitor changes to the ISs that may impact the security posture and the risk to the IS and its environment of operation (including the identification of new threats and vulnerabilities or other conditions that may impact the security state of the system). If changes occur, update the potential impact levels and inform the AO to determine if reauthorization is necessary.

8-302. Operational Controls. Operational controls are methods primarily implemented and executed by people (as opposed to systems) to improve system security. Contractors will apply the following Operational Control measures:

   a. **Personnel Security.**

     (1) Individuals occupying positions of responsibility for classified ISs meet the security criteria established for those positions;

     (2) Classified Information and ISs are protected during and after personnel actions, such as resignations, retirements, terminations, transfers, or loss of access to the system for cause, or the individual no longer has a reason to access the IS; in such circumstances, the individual's user ID and its authentication will be disabled or removed from the system and the account.

     (3) The contractor is required to review audit logs in accordance with CSA-provided

guidance, as a component of its continuous monitoring to determine if there are any personnel failing to comply with security policies and procedures and taking appropriate administrative actions. In addition, when circumstances warrant, the contractor will review audit logs, more immediately, if necessary, for inappropriate activity and employ appropriate administrative actions for personnel failing to comply with security policies and procedures.

b. **Physical and Environmental Protection.**

(1) Limit physical access into ISs operating environments to authorized individuals in accordance with reference (b).

(2) Protect the physical plant and support infrastructure for ISs.

(3) Provide supporting utilities for ISs, protect ISs against environmental hazards, and provide appropriate environmental controls in facilities containing ISs, when required by contract.

c. **Contingency Planning**. When contractually required, contractors will establish, maintain, and effectively implement plans for emergency response, backup operations, and post-disaster recovery operations for ISs to ensure the availability of critical information and continuity of operations.

d. **Configuration Management**. Contractors will:

(1) Establish and maintain baseline configurations and IS inventories (including hardware, software, firmware, and documentation) throughout the life cycles of these classified systems.

(2) Establish and enforce security configuration settings for information technology products employed in classified ISs, as prescribed by CSA guidelines.

e. **Maintenance**

(1) Perform necessary maintenance on classified ISs, including patch management.

(2) Provide effective controls on the tools, techniques, mechanisms, and personnel used to conduct classified ISs maintenance.

f. **Classified ISs and Information Integrity**

(1) Provide protection from malicious code at appropriate locations within classified ISs.

(2) Monitor IS security alerts and advisories that are accessible to contractors and take appropriate corrective action.

(3) Implement corrective measures to vulnerabilities identified by the GCA or CSA.

g. **Media Protection**

(1) Mark, label, and protect ISs media to the level of authorization until an appropriate classification review is conducted and resultant classification determination is made.

(2) Limit access to information on classified ISs media to authorized users.

(3) Sanitize or destroy ISs media before disposal or release for reuse in accordance with procedures established by the CSA.

h. **Trusted Downloading.** When contractor program management determines that there is a valid requirement to perform trusted downloading procedures for moving media from a high to lower security domain (e.g., TOP SECRET to SECRET; SECRET to Unclassified), the contractor must follow established procedures approved by the CSA. If conditions exist that prevent the use of CSA established trusted download procedures, alternate technical and administrative procedures must be documented, reviewed, tested, and certified to work by the ISSM. The AO may require the ISSM to submit the alternate procedures to the GCA for endorsement before the AO makes a decision whether to approve the use of the alternate procedures. Performing the alternative approved procedures is considered an alternate trusted download.

i. **Incident Response**

(1) Implement CSA-provided auditing processes and procedures in order to detect security incidents involving ISs.

(2) Report immediately any such incidents to the CSA.

(3) Respond to and mitigate incidents in accordance with CSA guidance.

j. Awareness and Training. The contractor will ensure personnel are adequately trained to carry out their assigned information security-related duties and responsibilities. When the results of the CSA's oversight indicate deficiencies in training or technical competence on the part of the ISSM or ISSO, the contractor will take appropriate corrective action.

8-303. Technical Controls. Technical controls focus on security controls that the computer system executes. The controls can provide automated protection for unauthorized access or misuse; facilitate detection of security violations; and support security requirements for applications and data. Contractors will apply the following technical control measures:

a. **Identification and Authentication.** Contractors will identify ISs users, processes acting on behalf of users, or devices and then will authenticate (or verify) the identities of those users, processes, or devices, as a prerequisite to allowing access to ISs. The CSA will provide direction on the length and content of passwords.

b. **Access Control.** Contractors will limit ISs access to authorized users, processes acting on behalf of authorized users, or authorized devices (including other ISs). Access must be limited to the types of transactions and functions that authorized users are permitted to exercise.

c. **Audit and Accountability**

(1) Create, protect, and retain ISs audit records to the extent needed to enable the monitoring, review and analysis, investigation, and reporting of unlawful, unauthorized, or inappropriate ISs activity.

(2) Uniquely trace the actions of individual ISs users so they can be held accountable for their actions.

d. **System and Communications Protection**

(1) Monitor, control, and protect organizational communications (i.e., information transmitted or received by the IS) at the external boundaries and key internal boundaries of the IS.

(2) Employ architectural designs, software development techniques, and systems engineering principles that promote effective information security.

8-304. Special Categories. Several categories of ISs (e.g., tactical, embedded ISs, or special purpose systems) can be adequately secured with compensating security controls. Compensating security controls cover the management, operational, or technical controls of the ISs. Compensating security controls, which provide equivalent or comparable ISs protection, may be employed in lieu of prescribed security control baselines when approved by the CSA.

a. The contractor will select the compensating controls from those described in the CSA-provided guideline set of security controls, and provide to the AO a complete rationale and justification for how the compensating controls provide an equivalent security capability or level of protection for the ISs.

b. The AO assesses the risk of operating the special categories ISs with the contractor's recommended set of compensating security controls. If the AO determines the risk is too high, the AO may require the contractor to request GCA acknowledgement that the GCA understands the risk associated with implementation of the contractor's proposed set of compensating security controls. Should the GCA also determine the risk is too high, it may recommend alternate or additional compensating security controls to the contractor and the AO, or recommend that the AO not authorize the system in its present security configuration.

c. The contractor may also obtain additional compensating controls from the GCA, if recommended by the GCA.

d. The contractor then resubmits to the AO for a final authorization decision, including the GCA's acknowledgement decision in accordance with paragraph 8-304b of this chapter with the contractor's initial set of compensating security controls. The contractor must also include the GCA's additional recommended compensating controls, if any were provided, in accordance with paragraph 8-304c of this chapter.

e. **Tactical, Embedded, Data-acquisition, Legacy, and Special-purpose Systems.** Tactical, embedded, data-acquisition, legacy, and special-purpose systems are special categories of systems requiring alternative set of controls not readily available in typical systems. Some ISs are incapable of alteration by users and are designed and implemented to provide a very limited set of predetermined functions. These systems are considered members of a special category, as are data-acquisition systems and other special-purpose test type systems. If an IS meets the criteria of a legacy IS (i.e., incapable of meeting the baseline security control requirements), authorization for continued use of a legacy IS may be granted when the benefits of upgrading the IS to meet baseline security controls do not outweigh the benefits of the additional controls and continued technological enhancements.

f. **Mobile Systems.** Mobile systems may be periodically relocated to another cleared contractor facility or government site. A mobile system may be a complete system or components of a larger more complex system. Special procedures are required to document applicability, control and account for the movement, operations, and security of systems that are relocated to alternative locations. When a mobile system requires relocation, the contractor must provide the CSA with sufficient notice before the date of relocation. The contractor must submit to the CSA a mobile processing plan that addresses all aspects of security and includes secure movement, physical security, and operations at the new location before relocation.

CHAPTER 9
Special Requirements

Section 1. RD, FRD, and Transclassified Foreign Nuclear Information (TFNI)

9-100. General. See Appendix D, "NISPOM Supplement" of this Manual.

Section 2. DOD Critical Nuclear Weapon Design Information (CNWDI)

9-200. General. This section contains the special requirements for protection of CNWDI.

9-201. Background. CNWDI is a DoD category of TOP SECRET RD or SECRET RD that reveals the theory of operation or design of the components of a thermonuclear or fission bomb, warhead, demolition munition, or test device. Specifically excluded is information concerning arming, fuzing, and firing systems; limited life components; and total contained quantities of fissionable, fusionable, and high explosive materials by type. Among these excluded items are the components that DoD personnel set, maintain, operate, test or replace. The sensitivity of DoD CNWDI is such that access shall be granted to the absolute minimum number of employees who require it for the accomplishment of assigned responsibilities on a classified contract. Because of the importance of such information, special requirements have been established for its control. DoD Instruction 5210.2 (reference (q)) establishes these controls in DoD.

9-202. Briefings. Prior to having access to DoD CNWDI, employees shall be briefed on its sensitivity by the FSO or his or her alternate. (The FSO will be initially briefed by a Government representative.) The briefing shall include the definition of DoD CNWDI, a reminder of the extreme sensitivity of the information, and an explanation of the individual's continuing responsibility for properly safeguarding DoD CNWDI, and for ensuring that dissemination is strictly limited to other personnel who have been authorized for access and have a need-to-know for the particular information. The briefing shall also be tailored to cover any special local requirements. Upon termination of access to DoD CNWDI, the employee shall be given an oral debriefing.

9-203. Markings. In addition to any other required markings, CNWDI material shall be clearly marked, "Critical Nuclear Weapon Design Information-DoD Instruction 5210.2 Applies." As a minimum, CNWDI documents shall show such markings on the cover or first page. Portions of documents that contain CNWDI shall be marked with an (N) or (CNWDI) following the classification of the portion; for example, TS(RD)(N) or TS(RD)(CNWDI).

9-204. Subcontractors. Contractors shall not disclose CNWDI to subcontractors without the prior written approval of the GCA. This approval may be included in a Contract Security Classification Specification, other contract-related document, or by separate correspondence.

9-205. Transmission Outside the Facility. Transmission outside the contractor's facility is authorized only to the GCA, or to a subcontractor as described in paragraph 9-204 above. Any other transmission must be approved by the GCA. Prior to transmission to another cleared facility, the contractor shall verify from the CSA that the facility has been authorized access to CNWDI. When CNWDI is transmitted to another facility, the inner wrapping shall be addressed to the personal attention of the FSO or his or her alternate, and in addition to any other prescribed markings, the inner wrapping shall be marked: "Critical Nuclear Weapon Design Information-DoD Instruction 5210.2 Applies." Similarly, transmissions addressed to the GCA or other U.S. Government agency shall bear on the inner wrapper the marking "Critical Nuclear Weapon Design Information-DoD Instruction 5210.2 Applies."

9-206. Records. Contractors shall annotate CNWDI access in the CSA-designated database for all employees who have been authorized access to CNWDI.

9-207. Weapon Data. That portion of RD or FRD that concerns the design, manufacture, or utilization (including theory, development, storage, characteristics, performance, and effects) of atomic weapons or atomic weapon components and nuclear explosive devices is called Weapon Data and it has special protection provisions. Weapon Data is divided into Sigma categories the protection of which is prescribed by DOE Order *452.8* (reference (r)). However, certain Weapon Data has been re-categorized as CNWDI and is protected as described in this section.

Section 3. Intelligence Information

9-300. General. National intelligence is under the jurisdiction and control of the DNI, who establishes security policy for the protection of national intelligence and intelligence sources, methods, and activities. In addition to the guidance in this Manual, contractors shall follow IC directives, policy guidance, standards, and specifications for the protection of classified national intelligence and SCI. Contractors are not authorized to further disclose or release classified national intelligence and SCI (including to a subcontractor) without prior written authorization of the originating IC element.

Section 4. Communications Security (COMSEC)

9-400. General. This section was prepared by NSA. The procedures in this section pertaining to COMSEC information shall apply to contractors when the contractor requires the use of COMSEC systems in the performance of a contract; the contractor is required to install, maintain, or operate COMSEC equipment for the U.S. Government; or the contractor is required to accomplish research, development, or production of COMSEC systems, COMSEC equipment, or related COMSEC material.

9-401. Instructions. Specific requirements for the management and safeguarding of COMSEC material in industry are established in the COMSEC material control and operating procedures provided to the custodian of each industrial COMSEC account by the agency Central Office of Record (COR) responsible for establishing the account. Such procedures that are above the baseline requirements detailed in the other sections of this manual shall be contractually mandated.

9-402. Clearance and Access Requirements

a. Before a COMSEC account can be established and a contractor may receive or possess COMSEC material accountable to a COR, individuals occupying the positions of FSO, COMSEC Account Manager, and Alternate COMSEC Account Manager must have a final PCL appropriate for the material to be held in the account. COMSEC Account Managers and Alternate COMSEC Account Managers having access to operational TOP SECRET keying material marked as CRYPTOGRAPHIC (CRYPTO) must have a final security clearance based upon an SSBI current within five years. This requirement does not apply to contractors using only data transfer devices and seed key.

b. Before disclosure of COMSEC information to a contractor, GCAs must first verify with the CSA that appropriate COMSEC procedures are in place at the contractor facility. If procedures are not in place, the GCA shall provide a written request and justification to the CSA to establish COMSEC procedures and a COMSEC account, if appropriate, at the facility and to conduct the initial COMSEC or Cryptographic Access briefings for the FSO and COMSEC account personnel.

c. Access to COMSEC information by a contractor requires a final FCL and a government-issued final PCL at the appropriate level; however, an Interim TOP SECRET FCL or PCL is valid for access to COMSEC at the SECRET and CONFIDENTIAL levels.

d. If a COMSEC account will be required, the Contract Security Classification Specification shall contain a statement regarding the establishment of a COMSEC account as appropriate.

9-403. Establishing a COMSEC Account

a. When COMSEC material which is accountable to a COR is to be provided, acquired or produced under a contract, the contracting officer shall inform the contractor that a COMSEC account must be established. The contractor shall forward the names of U.S. citizen employees who will serve as the COMSEC Account Manager and Alternate COMSEC Account Manager to the CSA. The CSA shall forward the names of the FSO, COMSEC Account Manager, and Alternate COMSEC Account Manager, along with a contractual requirement for the establishment of a COMSEC Account (using DD Form 254, "Contract Security Classification Specification ") to the appropriate COR, with a copy to the GCA, indicating that the persons have been cleared and COMSEC has been briefed.

b. The COR will then establish the COMSEC account and will notify the CSA that the account has been established.

c. An individual may be appointed as the COMSEC Account Manager or Alternate COMSEC Account Manager for more than one account only when approved by each COR concerned.

9-404. COMSEC Briefing and Debriefing Requirements

a. All contractor employees who require access to classified COMSEC information in the performance of their duties shall be briefed before access is granted. Depending on the nature of COMSEC access required, either a COMSEC briefing or a Cryptographic Access Briefing will be given. The FSO, the COMSEC Account Manager, and the Alternate COMSEC Account Manager shall be briefed by a government representative or their designee. Other contractor employees shall be briefed by the FSO, the COMSEC Account personnel, or other individual designated by the FSO. The purpose of the briefing is to ensure that the contractor understands:

(1) The unique nature of COMSEC information and its unusual sensitivity,

(2) The special security requirements for the handling and protection of COMSEC information, and

(3) The penalties prescribed in Title 18, U.S.C., §§ 793, 794, and 798 (reference (s)) for willful disclosure of COMSEC information.

b. COMSEC debriefings are not required.

c. The contractor shall maintain a record of all COMSEC briefings as specified by the appropriate COR.

9-405. CRYPTO Access Briefing and Debriefing Requirements

a. U.S. classified CRYPTO information is defined as:

(1) TOP SECRET and SECRET, CRYPTO, key and authenticators that are designated CRYPTO, and

(2) CRYPTO media that embody, describe, or implement classified CRYPTO logic; this includes full maintenance manuals, CRYPTO descriptions, drawings of a CRYPTO logic, specifications describing a CRYPTO logic, CRYPTO computer software, or any other media which may be specifically identified.

b. U.S. classified CRYPTO information does not include seed key or CCI.

c. A contractor's employee may be granted access to U.S. classified CRYPTO information only if the employee:

(1) Is a U.S. citizen;

(2) Has a final government-issued security clearance appropriate to the classification of the U.S. CRYPTO information to be accessed;

(3) Has a valid need-to-know to perform duties for, or on behalf of, the U.S. Government;

(4) Receives a security briefing appropriate to the U.S. classified CRYPTO information to be accessed;

(5) Acknowledges the granting of access by executing Section I of Secretary of Defense Form (SD) 572, Cryptographic Access Certification and Termination; and

(6) Where so directed by a U.S. Government Department or Agency head, acknowledges the possibility of being subject to a non-lifestyle, CI-scope polygraph examination that shall be administered in accordance with department or agency directives and applicable law.

d. An employee granted access to CRYPTO information shall be debriefed and execute Section II of the SD 572 not later than 90 days from the date access is no longer required.

e. The contractor shall maintain the SD 572 for a minimum of three years following the debriefing.

f. CRYPTO access briefings fully meet the requirements of paragraph 9-405 of this Manual for COMSEC briefings.

9-406. Destruction and Disposition of COMSEC Material. The appropriate COR shall provide directions to the contractor when accountable COMSEC material is to be destroyed. These directions may be provided in superseding editions of publications or by specific instructions.

9-407. Subcontracting COMSEC Work. Subcontracts requiring the disclosure of classified COMSEC information shall be awarded only upon the written approval of the GCA.

9-408. Unsolicited Proposals. Any unsolicited proposal for a COMSEC system, equipment, development, or study that may be submitted by a contractor to a government agency shall be forwarded to the Director, Information Assurance, NSA, Fort George G. Meade, MD 20755-6000, for review and appropriate follow-up action.

CHAPTER 10
International Security Requirements

Section 1. General and Background Information

10-100. General. This Chapter provides policy and procedures governing the control of classified information in international programs.

10-101. Applicable Federal Laws. The transfer of articles and services and related technical data to a foreign person, within or outside the U.S., or the movement of such material or information to any destination outside the legal jurisdiction of the U.S. constitutes an export. Depending on the nature of the articles or data, most exports are governed by the Arms Export Control Act (AECA) (reference (t)), the Export Administration Act (EAA) (reference (u)), and reference (c).

10-102. Bilateral Security Agreements. Bilateral security agreements are negotiated with various foreign governments. Confidentiality requested by some foreign governments prevents a listing of the countries that have executed these agreements.

a. The General Security Agreement, negotiated through diplomatic channels, requires that each government provide to the classified information provided by the other substantially the same degree of protection as the releasing government. The Agreement contains provisions concerning limits on the use of each government's information, including restrictions on third party transfers and proprietary rights. It does not commit governments to share classified information, nor does it constitute authority to release classified material to that government. It satisfies, in part, the eligibility requirements of reference (t) concerning the agreement of the recipient foreign government to protect U.S. classified defense articles and technical data. (The General Security Agreement also is known as a General Security of Information Agreement and General Security of Military Information Agreement. The title and scope are different, depending on the year the particular agreement was signed.)

b. Industrial security agreements have been negotiated with certain foreign governments that identify the procedures to be used when foreign government information is provided to industry. The Office of the Under Secretary of Defense (Policy) negotiates Industrial Security Agreements as an Annex to the General Security Agreement and the Director, DSS, has been delegated authority to implement the provisions of the Industrial Security Agreements. The Director of Security, NRC, negotiates and implements these agreements for the NRC.

Section 2. Disclosure of U.S. Information to Foreign Interests

10-200. Authorization for Disclosure. Disclosure guidance will be provided by the GCA. Disclosure authorization may be in the form of an export license, a technical assistance agreement, a manufacturing license agreement, a letter of authorization from the U.S. Government licensing authority, or an exemption to the export authorization requirements. Disclosure guidance provided for a previous contract or program shall not be used unless the contractor is so instructed in writing by the GCA or the licensing authority. Classified information normally will be authorized for disclosure and export as listed below:

a. Government-to-Government International Agreements. Classified information shall not be disclosed until agreements are signed by the participating governments and disclosure guidance and security arrangements are established. The export of technical data pursuant to such agreements may be exempt from licensing requirements of the International Traffic in Arms Regulation (ITAR) (reference (v).

b. Symposia, Seminars, Exhibitions, and Conferences. Appropriately cleared foreign nationals may participate in classified gatherings if authorized by the Head of the U.S. Government Agency that authorizes the conduct of the conference.

c. Foreign Visits. Disclosure of classified information shall be limited to that specific information authorized in connection with an approved visit request or export authorization.

d. Temporary Exports. Classified articles (including articles that require the use of classified information for operation) exported for demonstration purposes shall remain under U.S. control. The request for export authorization shall include a description of the arrangements that have been made in-country for U.S. control of the demonstrations and secure storage under U.S. Government control.

10-201. Direct Commercial Arrangements. The disclosure of classified information may be authorized pursuant to a direct commercial sale only if the proposed disclosure supports a U.S. or foreign government procurement requirement, a government contract, or an international agreement. A direct commercial arrangement includes sales, loans, leases, or grants of classified items, including sales under a government agency sales financing program. If a

proposed disclosure is in support of a foreign government requirement, the contractor should consult with U.S. in-country officials (normally the U.S. Security Assistance/Armaments Cooperation Office or Commercial Counselor). An export authorization is required before a contractor makes a proposal to a foreign interest that involves the eventual disclosure of U.S. classified information. The contractor should obtain the concurrence of the GCA before submitting an export authorization request.

10-202. Contract Security Provisions.

a. When a U.S. contractor is authorized to award a subcontract or enter into a Manufacturing License Agreement, Technical Assistance Agreement, or other direct commercial arrangement with a foreign contractor that will involve classified information, security provisions will be incorporated in the subcontract document or agreement and security classification guidance via a Contract Security Classification Specification will be provided. A copy of the signed contract with the provisions and the classification guidance shall be provided to the CSA. If the export authorization specifies that additional security arrangements are necessary for performance on the contract, contractor developed arrangements shall be incorporated in appropriate provisions in the contract or in a separate security document.

b. The contractor shall prepare and maintain a written record that identifies the originator or source of classified information that will be used in providing defense articles or services to foreign customers. The contractor shall maintain this listing with the contractor's record copy of the pertinent export authorization.

c. Security provisions, substantially as shown below, shall be included in all contracts and subcontracts involving classified information that are awarded to foreign contractors.

(1) All classified information and material furnished or generated under this contract shall be protected as follows:

(a) The recipient will not release the information or material to a third-country government, person, or firm without the prior approval of the releasing government.

(b) The recipient will afford the information and material a degree of protection equivalent to that afforded it by the releasing government; and

(c) The recipient will not use the information and material for other than the purpose for which it was furnished without the prior written consent of the releasing government.

(2) Classified information and material furnished or generated under this contract shall be transferred through government channels or other channels specified in writing by the Governments of the United States and (insert applicable country) and only to persons who have an appropriate security clearance and an official need for access to the information in order to perform on the contract.

(3) Classified information and material furnished under this contract will be remarked by the recipient with its government's equivalent security classification markings.

(4) Classified information and material generated under this contract must be assigned a security classification as specified by the contract security classification specifications provided with this contract.

(5) All cases in which it is known or there is reason to believe that classified information or material furnished or generated under this contract has been lost or disclosed to unauthorized persons shall be reported promptly and fully by the contractor to its government's security authorities.

(6) Classified information and material furnished or generated pursuant to this contract shall not be further provided to another potential contractor or subcontractor unless:

(a) A potential contractor or subcontractor which is located in the United States or (insert applicable country) has been approved for access to classified information and material by U.S. or (insert applicable country) security authorities; or,

(b) If located in a third country, prior written consent is obtained from the United States Government.

(7) Upon completion of the contract, all classified material furnished or generated pursuant to the contract will be returned to the U.S. contractor or be destroyed.

(8) The recipient contractor shall insert terms that substantially conform to the language of these provisions, including this one, in all subcontracts under this contract that involve access to classified information furnished or generated under this contract.

Section 3. Foreign Government Information (FGI)

10-300. General. The contractor shall notify the CSA when awarded contracts by a foreign interest that will involve access to classified information. The CSA shall administer oversight and ensure implementation of the security requirements of the contract on behalf of the foreign government, including the establishment of channels for the transfer of classified material.

10-301. Contract Security Requirements. The foreign entity that awards a classified contract is responsible for providing appropriate security classification guidance and any security requirements clauses. The failure of a foreign entity to provide classification guidance shall be reported to the CSA.

10-302. Marking Foreign Government Classified Material.

a. Foreign government classified information shall retain its original classification markings or shall be assigned a U.S. classification that provides a degree of protection at least equivalent to that required by the government entity that furnished the information. The equivalent U.S. classification and the country of origin shall be marked on the front and back in English.

10-303. Foreign Government RESTRICTED Information and "In Confidence" Information.

a. Some foreign governments have a fourth level of classification that does not correspond to an equivalent U.S. classification that is identified as RESTRICTED Information. In many cases, bilateral security agreements require RESTRICTED information to be protected as U.S. CONFIDENTIAL information.

b. Some foreign governments may have a category of unclassified information that is protected by law. This latter category is normally provided to other governments on the condition that the information is treated "In Confidence." The foreign government or international organization must state that the information is provided in confidence and that it must be protected from release. A provision of Title 10 of the U.S. Code (reference (w)) protects information provided "In Confidence" by foreign governments or international organizations to the Department of Defense which is not classified but meets special requirements stated in section 130c reference (w). This provision also applies to RESTRICTED information which is not required by a bilateral agreement to be protected as classified information. The contractor shall not disclose information protected by this statutory provision to anyone except personnel who require access to the information in connection with the contract.

c. It is the responsibility of the foreign entity that awards the contract to incorporate requirements for the protection and marking of RESTRICTED or "In Confidence" information in the contract. The contractor shall advise the CSA if requirements were not provided by the foreign entity.

10-304. Marking U.S. Documents Containing FGI

a. U.S. documents containing foreign government information shall be marked on the front, "THIS DOCUMENT CONTAINS (indicate country of origin) INFORMATION." In addition, the portions shall be marked to identify both the country and classification level, e.g., (UK-C); (GE-C). The "Derived From" line shall identify U.S. as well as foreign classification sources.

b. If the identity of the foreign government must be concealed, the front of the document shall be marked "THIS DOCUMENT CONTAINS FOREIGN GOVERNMENT INFORMATION;" paragraphs shall be marked FGI, together with the classification level, e.g., (FGI-C); and the "Derived From" line shall indicate FGI in addition to any U.S. source. The identity of the foreign government shall be maintained with the record copy of the document.

c. A U.S. document, marked as described herein, shall not be downgraded below the highest level of foreign government information contained in the document or be declassified without the written approval of the foreign government that originated the information. Recommendations concerning downgrading or declassification shall be submitted to the GCA or foreign government contracting authority, as applicable.

10-305. Marking Documents Prepared For Foreign Governments. Documents prepared for foreign governments that contain U.S. and foreign government information shall be marked as prescribed by the foreign government. In addition, they shall be marked on the front, "THIS DOCUMENT CONTAINS UNITED STATES CLASSIFIED INFORMATION."

Portions shall be marked to identify the U.S. classified information.

10-306. Storage and Control. Foreign government material shall be stored and access shall be controlled generally in the same manner as U.S. classified material of an equivalent classification. Foreign government material shall be stored in a manner that will avoid commingling with other material which may be accomplished by establishing separate files in a storage container.

10-307. Disclosure and Use Limitations. Foreign government information is provided by the foreign government to the United States. It shall not be disclosed to nationals of a third country, or to any other third party, or be used for other than the purpose for which it was provided without the prior written consent of the originating foreign government. Requests for other uses or further disclosure shall be submitted to the GCA for U.S. contracts, and through the CSA for direct commercial contracts. Approval of the request by the foreign government does not eliminate the requirement for the contractor to obtain an export authorization.

10-308. Transfer. Foreign government information shall be transferred within the U.S. and its territories using the same channels as specified by this Manual for U.S. classified information of an equivalent classification, except that non-cleared express overnight carriers shall not be used.

10-309. Reproduction. The reproduction of foreign government TOP SECRET information requires the written approval of the originating government.

10-310. Disposition. Foreign government information shall be destroyed on completion of the contract unless the contract specifically authorizes retention or return of the information to the GCA or foreign government that provided the information. TOP SECRET destruction must be witnessed and a destruction certificate executed and retained for 2 years.

10-311. Reporting of Improper Receipt of Foreign Government Material. The contractor shall report to the CSA the receipt of classified material from foreign interests that is not received through government channels.

10-312. Subcontracting

a. A U.S. contractor may award a subcontract that involves access to FGI to another U.S. contractor, except as described in subparagraph b, on verifying with the CSA that the prospective subcontractor has the appropriate FCL and storage capability. The contractor awarding a subcontract shall provide appropriate security classification guidance and incorporate the pertinent security provisions in the subcontract.

b. Subcontracts involving FGI shall not be awarded to a contractor in a third country or to a U.S. company with a limited FCL based on third-country ownership, control, or influence without the express written consent of the originating foreign government. The CSA will coordinate with the appropriate foreign government authorities.

Section 4. International Transfers

10-400. General. This section contains the procedures for international transfers of classified material. The requirements in this section do not apply to the transmission of classified material to U.S. Government activities outside the United States.

10-401. International Transfers of Classified Material

a. All international transfers of classified material shall take place through channels approved by both governments. Control of classified material must be maintained until the material is officially transferred to the intended recipient government through its designated government representative (DGR).

b. To ensure government control, written transmission instructions shall be prepared for all international transfers of classified material. Preparation of the instructions shall be the responsibility of the contractor for direct commercial arrangements, and the GCA for government arrangements.

c. The CSA shall be contacted at the earliest possible stage in deliberations that will lead to the international transfer of classified material. The CSA shall advise the contractor on the transfer arrangements, identify the recipient government's DGR, appoint a U.S. DGR, and ensure that the transportation plan prepared by the contractor or foreign government is adequate.

d. Requests for export authorizations that will involve the transfer of classified material shall be accompanied by a Department of State Form DSP-83, Non-Transfer and Use Certificate. The form shall be signed by an official of the responsible foreign government who has the authority to certify that the transfer is for government purposes and that the classified material will be protected in compliance with a government-approved security agreement.

10-402. Transfers of Freight

a. Transportation Plan (TP). A requirement to prepare a TP shall be included in each arrangement that involves the international transfer of classified material as freight. The TP shall describe arrangements for the secure shipment of the material from the point of origin to the ultimate destination. The U.S. and recipient government DGRs shall be identified in the TP as well as any requirement for an escort. The TP shall provide for security arrangements in the event the transfer cannot be made promptly. When there are to be repetitive shipments, a Notice of Classified Consignment will be used.

b. Government Agency Arrangements. Classified material to be furnished to a foreign government under such transactions normally will be shipped via government agency-arranged transportation and be transferred to the foreign government's DGR within the recipient government's territory. The government agency that executes the arrangement is responsible, in coordination with the recipient foreign government, for preparing a TP. When the point of origin is a U.S. contractor facility, the GCA shall provide the contractor a copy of the TP and the applicable Letter of Offer and Acceptance (LOA). If a freight forwarder is to be used in processing the shipment, the freight forwarder shall be provided a copy of the TP by the GCA.

c. Commercial Arrangements. The contractor shall prepare a TP in coordination with the receiving government. This requirement applies whether the material is to be moved by land, sea, or air, and applies to U.S. and foreign classified contracts. After the CSA approves the TP, it shall be forwarded to the recipient foreign government security authorities for final coordination and approval.

d. International Carriers. The international transfer of classified material shall be made using only ships, aircraft, or other carriers that:

(1) Are owned or chartered by the U.S Government or under U.S. registry,

(2) Are owned or chartered by or under the registry of the recipient government, or

(3) Are carriers other than those described that are expressly authorized to perform this function in writing by the Designated Security Authority of the GCA and the security authorities of the foreign government involved. This authority shall not be delegated and this exception may be authorized only when a carrier described in (1) or (2) above is not available and/or an urgent operational requirement dictates use of the exception.

10-403. Return of Material for Repair, Modification, or Maintenance. A foreign government or contractor may return classified material to a U.S. contractor for repair, modification, or maintenance. The approved methods of return shall be specified in either the GCA sales arrangement, the security requirements section of a direct commercial sales arrangement, or, in the case of material transferred as freight, in the original TP. The contractor, on receipt of notification that classified material is to be received, shall notify the applicable CSA.

10-404. Use of Freight Forwarders.

a. A commercial freight forwarder may be used to arrange for the international transfer of classified material as freight. The freight forwarder must be under contract to a government agency, U.S. contractor, or the recipient foreign government. The contract shall describe the specific functions to be performed by the freight forwarder. The responsibility for security and control of the classified material that is processed by freight forwarders remains with the U.S. Government until the freight is transferred to a DGR of the recipient government.

b. Only freight forwarders that have a valid FCL and storage capability at the appropriate level are eligible to take custody or possession of classified material for delivery as freight to foreign recipients. Freight forwarders that only process unclassified paperwork and make arrangements for the delivery of classified material to foreign recipients do not require an FCL.

10-405. Hand Carrying Classified Material. To meet contractual requirements, the CSA may authorize contractor employees to hand carry classified material outside the United States. SECRET is the highest level of classified material to be carried and it shall be of such size and weight that the courier can retain it in his or her possession at all times. The CSA shall ensure that the contractor has made necessary arrangements with U.S. airport security and customs officials and that security authorities of the receiving government approve the plan. If the transfer is under a contract or a bilateral or multinational government program, the request shall be approved in writing by the GCA. The CSA shall be notified by the contractor of a requirement under this section at least 5 work days in advance of the transfer. In addition:

a. The courier shall be a full-time, appropriately cleared employee of the dispatching contractor.

b. The courier shall be provided with a Courier Certificate that shall be consecutively numbered and be valid for one journey only. The journey may include more than one stop if approved by the CSA and secure Government storage has been arranged at each stop. The Courier Certificate shall be returned to the dispatching security officer immediately on completion of the journey.

c. Before commencement of each journey, the courier shall read and initial the Notes to the Courier attached to the Courier Certificate and sign the Courier Declaration. The Declaration shall be maintained by the FSO until completion of the next security inspection by the CSA.

d. The material shall be inventoried, and shall be wrapped and sealed in the presence of the U.S. DGR. The address of the receiving security office and the return address of the dispatching company security office shall be shown on the inner envelope or wrapping. The address of the receiving government's DGR shall be shown on the outer envelope or wrapping along with the return address of the dispatching office.

e. The dispatching company security office shall prepare three copies of a receipt based on the inventory and list the classified material involved. One copy of the receipt shall be retained by the dispatching company security office. The other two copies shall be packed with the classified material. The security office shall obtain a receipt for the sealed package from the courier.

f. The dispatching company security office shall provide the receiving security office with 24 work hours advance notification of the anticipated date and time of the courier's arrival and the identity of the courier. The receiving security office shall notify the dispatching company security office if the courier does not arrive within 8 hours of the expected time of arrival. The dispatching security office shall notify its DGR of any delay, unless officially notified otherwise of a change in the courier's itinerary.

g. The receiving DGR shall verify the contents of the consignment and shall sign the receipts enclosed in the consignment. One copy shall be returned to the courier. On return, the courier shall provide the executed receipt to the dispatching security office.

h. Throughout the journey, the consignment shall remain under the direct personal control of the courier. It shall not be left unattended at any time during the journey, in the transport being used, in hotel rooms, in cloakrooms, or other such location, and it may not be deposited in hotel safes, luggage lockers, or in luggage offices. In addition, envelopes and packages containing the classified material shall not be opened en route, unless required by customs or other government officials.

i. When inspection by government officials is unavoidable, the courier shall request that the officials provide written verification that they have opened the package. The courier shall notify the FSO as soon as possible. The FSO shall notify the U.S. DGR. If the inspecting officials are not of the same country as the dispatching security office, the designated security authority in the country whose officials inspected the consignment shall be notified by the CSA. Under no circumstances shall the classified consignment be handed over to customs or other officials for their custody.

j. When carrying classified material, the courier shall not travel by surface routes through third countries, except as authorized by the CSA. The courier shall travel only on carriers described in 10-402d, and travel direct routes between the U.S. and the destination.

10-406. Classified Material Receipts. There shall be a continuous chain of receipts to record international transfers of all classified material from the contractor through the U.S. DGR and the recipient DGR to the ultimate foreign recipient. The contractor shall retain an active suspense record until return of applicable receipts for the material. A copy of the external receipt that records the passing of custody of the package containing the classified material shall be retained by the contractor and each intermediate consignee in a suspense file until the receipt that is enclosed in the package is signed and returned. Follow-up action shall be initiated through the CSA if the signed receipt is not returned within 45 days.

10-407. Contractor Preparations for International Transfers Pursuant to Commercial and User Agency Sales. The contractor shall be responsible for the following preparations to facilitate international transfers:

a. Ensure that each party to be involved in the transfer is identified in the applicable contract or agreement, and in the license application or letter request.

b. Notify the appropriate U.S. DGR when the material is ready.

c. Provide documentation or written certification by an empowered official (as defined in the ITAR) to the U.S. DGR to verify that the classified shipment is within the limitations of the pertinent export authorization or an authorized exemption to the export authorization requirements, or is within the limitations of the pertinent GCA contract.

d. Have the classified shipment ready for visual review and verification by the DGR. As a minimum this will include:

(1) Preparing the packaging materials, address labels, and receipts for review.

(2) Marking the contents with the appropriate U.S. classification or the equivalent foreign government classification, downgrading, and declassification markings, as applicable.

(3) Ensuring that shipping documents (including, as appropriate, the Shipper's Export Declaration) include the name and contact information for the CSA that validates the license or letter authorization, and the FSO or designee for the particular transfer.

(4) Sending advance notification of the shipment to the CSA, the recipient, and to the freight forwarder, if applicable. The notification will require that the recipient confirm receipt of the shipment or provide notice to the contractor if the shipment is not received in accordance with the prescribed shipping schedule.

10-408. Transfers Pursuant to an ITAR Exemption

a. The contractor shall provide to the DGR valid documentation (i.e., license, Letter of Offer and Acceptance, or agreement) to verify the export authorization for classified technical data or certain defense articles to be transferred under an exemption to reference (v). The documentation shall include a copy of the Form DSP-83 associated with the original export authorization.

b. Classified technical data or certain defense articles to be exported pursuant to reference (v) exemptions 125.4(b)(1), 125.4(c), 125.5, 126.4(a), or 126.4(c) shall be supported by a written authorization signed by an Authorized Exemption Official or Exemption Certifying Official who has been appointed by the responsible Principal Disclosure Authority of the GCA. A copy of the authorization shall be provided by the contractor through the CSA to the State Department, Directorate of Defense Trade Controls (DDTC).

c. Exports shall not be permitted under a Manufacturing License or Technical Assistance Agreement for which the authorization has expired.

Section 5. International Visits and Control of Foreign Nationals

10-500. General. This section describes the procedures that the United States and foreign governments have established to control international visits to their organizations and cleared contractor facilities.

10-501. International Visits

a. The contractor shall establish procedures to monitor international visits by their employees and visits or assignments to their facilities of foreign nationals to ensure that the disclosure of, and access to, export-controlled articles and related information are limited to those that are approved by an export authorization.

b. Visit authorizations shall not be used to employ or otherwise acquire the services of foreign nationals that require access to export-controlled information. An export authorization is required for such situations.

10-502. Types and Purpose of International Visits. Visit requests are necessary to make administrative arrangements and disclosure decisions, and obtain security assurances. There are three types of international visits:

a. **One-time Visits.** A visit for a single, short-term occasion (normally less than 30 days) for a specified purpose.

b. **Recurring Visits.** Intermittent, recurring visits over a specified period of time, normally up to 1 year in duration, in support of a Government-approved arrangement, such as an agreement, contract, or license. By agreement of the governments, the term of the authorization may be for the duration of the arrangement, subject to annual review, and validation.

c. **Extended Visits.** A single visit for an extended period of time, normally up to 1 year, in support of an agreement, contract, or license.

10-503. Emergency Visits. Some foreign governments will accept a visit request submitted within 7 calendar days of the proposed visit for an "emergency visit." To qualify as an emergency visit, the visit must relate to a specific Government-approved contract, international agreement or announced request for proposal, and failure to make the visit could be reasonably expected to seriously jeopardize performance on the contract or program, or

result in the loss of a contract opportunity. Emergency visits are approved only as a single, one-time visit. The requester should coordinate the emergency visit in advance with the person to be visited and ensure that the complete name, position, address, and telephone number of the person and a knowledgeable foreign government point of contact are provided in the visit request, along with the identification of the contract, agreement, or program and the justification for submission of the emergency visit request.

10-504. Requests for Recurring Visits. Recurring visit authorizations should be requested at the beginning of each program. After approval of the request, individual visits may be arranged directly with the security office of the location to be visited subject to 3 working days advance notice.

10-505. Amendments. Visit requests that have been approved or are being processed may be amended only to change, add, or delete names and change dates. Amendments requesting earlier dates than originally specified shall not be accepted. Emergency visit authorizations shall not be amended.

10-506. Visits Abroad by U.S. Contractors. Many foreign governments require the submission of a visit request for all visits to a government facility or a cleared contractor facility, even though classified information may not be involved. They also require that the requests be received a specified number of days in advance of the visit. These lead times for North Atlantic Treaty Organization (NATO) countries are in Appendix B. An export authorization must be obtained if export controlled technical data is to be disclosed or, if information to be divulged is related to a classified U.S. Government program, unless the disclosure of the information is covered by an ITAR exemption. Visit request procedures are outlined as follows:

a. **Request Format.** The visit request format is contained in Appendix B. The visit request shall be forwarded to the security official designated by the CSA. The host for the visit should coordinate the visit in advance with appropriate government authorities who are required to approve the visit. It is the visitor's responsibility to ensure that such coordination has occurred.

b. **Government Agency Programs.** When contractor employees are to visit foreign government facilities or foreign contractors on U.S. Government orders in support of a government contract or agreement, a visit request shall be submitted by the contractor.

10-507. Visits by Foreign Nationals to U.S. Contractor Facilities. Requests for visits by foreign nationals to U.S. contractor facilities that will involve the disclosure of (a) classified information, (b) unclassified information related to a U.S. Government classified program, or (c) plant visits covered by Section 125.5 of reference (v) shall be processed through the sponsoring foreign government (normally the visitor's embassy) to the U.S. Government agency for approval. (NOTE: Requests for visits by foreign nationals that involve only commercial programs and related unclassified information may be submitted directly to the contractor. It is the contractor's responsibility to ensure that an export authorization is obtained, if applicable.) As described below, the U.S. government agency may approve or deny the request or decline to render a decision.

a. **Government-Approved Visits.** U.S. Government-approved visits constitute an exemption to the export licensing provisions of the ITAR. U.S. Government approved visits shall not be used to avoid the export licensing requirements for commercial initiatives. When the cognizant U.S. Government agency approves a visit, the notification of approval shall contain instructions on the level and scope of classified and unclassified information authorized for disclosure, as well as any limitations. Final acceptance of the visit shall be subject to the concurrence of the contractor who shall notify the U.S. Government agency when a visit is not desired.

b. **Visit Request Denials.** If the U.S. Government agency does not approve the disclosure of the information related to the proposed visit, it will deny the visit request. The requesting government and the contractor to be visited shall be advised of the reason for the denial. The contractor may accept the visitor(s). However, only information that is in the public domain may be disclosed.

c. **Non-Sponsorship.** The U.S. Government agency will decline to render a decision on a visit request that is not in support of a U.S. Government program. A declination notice indicating that the visit is not government-approved (i.e., the visit is non-sponsored) shall be furnished to the requesting foreign government with an information copy to the U.S. contractor to be visited. A declination notice does not preclude the visit, provided the contractor has, or obtains, an export authorization for the information

involved and, if classified information is involved, has been notified that the requesting foreign government has provided the required security assurance of the proposed visitor to the U.S. Government agency in the original visit request. It shall be the responsibility of the contractor to consult applicable export regulations to determine licensing requirements regarding the disclosure of export controlled information during such visits by foreign nationals.

d. **Access by Foreign Visitors to Classified Information.** The contractor shall establish procedures to ensure that foreign visitors are not afforded access to classified information and other export-controlled technical data except as authorized by an export license, approved visit request, or other exemption to the licensing requirements. The contractor shall not inform the foreign visitor of the scope of access authorized or of the limitations imposed by the government. Foreign visitors shall not be given custody of classified material except when they are acting as official couriers of their government and the CSA authorizes the transfer.

e. **Visitor Records.** The contractor shall maintain a record of foreign visitors when the visit involves access to classified information. These records shall be maintained for 1 year.

f. **Visits to Subsidiaries.** A visit request authorization for a visit to any element of a corporate family may be used for visits to other divisions or subsidiaries within the same corporate family provided disclosures are for the same purpose and the information to be disclosed does not exceed the parameters of the approved visit request.

10-508. Control of Access by On-Site Foreign Nationals

a. Extended visits and assignments of foreign nationals to contractor facilities shall be authorized only when it is essential that the foreign national be at the facility pursuant to a contract or government agreement (e.g., joint venture, liaison representative to a joint or multinational program, or direct commercial sale).

b. If the foreign national will require access to export-controlled information related to, or derived from, a U.S. Government classified contract, the contractor shall obtain the written consent of the GCA before making a commitment to accept the proposed visit or assignment. A copy of the written consent shall be included with the request for export authorization, when such authorization is required.

c. The applicable CSA shall be notified in advance of all extended visits and assignments of foreign nationals to cleared contractor facilities. The notification shall include a copy of the approved visit authorization or the U.S. Government export authorization, and the TCP if applicable.

d. Classified U.S. and foreign government material in a U.S. contractor facility is to remain under U.S. contractor custody and control and is subject to inspection by the FSO and the CSA. This does not preclude a foreign visitor from being furnished a security container for the temporary storage of classified material, consistent with the purpose of the visit or assignment, provided the CSA approves and responsibility for the container and its contents remains with the U.S. contractor. Exceptions to this policy may be approved on a case-by-case basis by the CSA for the storage of foreign government classified information furnished to the visitor by the visitor's government through government channels. Exceptions shall be approved in advance in writing by the CSA and agreed to by the visitor's government. The agreed procedures shall be included in the contractor's TCP, shall require the foreign nationals to provide receipts for the material, and shall include an arrangement for the CSA to ensure compliance, including provisions for the CSA to inspect and inventory the material.

10-509. TCP. A TCP is required to control access by foreign nationals assigned to, or employed by, cleared contractor facilities unless the CSA determines that procedures already in place at the contractor's facility are adequate. The TCP shall contain procedures to control access for all export-controlled information. A sample of a TCP may be obtained from the CSA.

10-510. Security and Export Control Violations Involving Foreign Nationals. Any violation of administrative security procedures or export control regulations that would subject classified information to possible compromise by foreign visitors or foreign national employees shall be reported to the CSA.

Section 6. Contractor Operations Abroad

10-600. General. This section sets forth requirements governing contractor operations abroad, including PCLs for U.S. contractor employees assigned outside the United States and their access to classified information.

10-601. Access by Contractor Employees Assigned Outside the United States.

a. Contractor employees assigned outside the United States, its possessions or territories may have access to classified information in connection with performance on a specified United States, NATO, or foreign government classified contract.

b. The assignment of an employee who is a foreign national, including intending citizens, outside the United States on programs that will involve access to classified information is prohibited and negates the basis on which an LAA may have been provided to such employee.

c. A consultant shall not be assigned outside the United States with responsibilities requiring access to classified information.

10-602. Storage, Custody, and Control of Classified Information Abroad by Employees of a U.S. Contractor.

a. The storage, custody, and control of classified information required by a U.S. contractor employee abroad is the responsibility of the U.S. Government. Therefore, the storage of classified information by contractor employees at any location abroad that is not under U.S. Government control is prohibited. The storage may be at a U.S. military facility, a U.S. Embassy or Consulate, or other location occupied by a U.S. Government organization.

b. A contractor employee may be furnished a security container to temporarily store classified material at a U.S. Government agency overseas location. The decision to permit a contractor to temporarily store classified information must be approved in writing by the senior security official for the U.S. Government host organization.

c. A contractor employee may be permitted to temporarily remove classified information from an overseas U.S. Government-controlled facility when necessary for the performance of a GCA contract or pursuant to an approved export authorization. The responsible U.S. Government security official at the U.S. Government facility shall verify that the contractor has an export authorization or other written U.S. Government approval to have the material, verify the need for the material to be removed from the facility, and brief the employee on handling procedures. In such cases, the contractor employee shall sign a receipt for the classified material. Arrangements shall also be made with the U.S. Government custodian for the return and storage of the classified material during non-duty hours. Violations of this policy shall be reported to the applicable CSA by the security office at the U.S. Government facility.

d. A contractor employee shall not store classified information at overseas divisions or subsidiaries of U.S. companies incorporated or located in a foreign country. (NOTE: The divisions or subsidiaries may possess classified information that has been transferred to the applicable foreign government through government-to-government channels pursuant to an approved export authorization or other written U.S. Government authorization. Access to this classified information at such locations by a U.S. contractor employee assigned abroad by the parent facility on a visit authorization in support of a foreign government contract or subcontract, is governed by the laws and regulations of the country in which the division or subsidiary is registered or incorporated. The division or subsidiary that has obtained the information from the foreign government shall provide the access.)

e. U.S. contractor employees assigned to foreign government or foreign contractor facilities under a direct commercial sales arrangement will be subject to the host-nation's industrial security policies.

10-603. Transmission of Classified Material to Employees Abroad. The transmission of classified material to a cleared contractor employee located outside the United States shall be through U.S. Government channels. If the material is to be used for other than U.S. Government purposes, an export authorization is required and a copy of the authorization, validated by the DGR, shall accompany the material. The material shall be addressed to a U.S. military organization or other U.S. Government organization (e.g., an embassy). The U.S. government organization abroad shall be responsible for custody and control of the material.

10-604. Security Briefings. An employee being assigned outside the United States shall be briefed on the security requirements of his or her assignment, including the handling, disclosure, and storage of classified information overseas.

Section 7. NATO Information Security Requirements

10-700. General. This section provides the security requirements needed to comply with the procedures established by the U.S. Security Authority for NATO (USSAN) for safeguarding NATO information provided to U.S. industry.

10-701. Classification Levels. NATO has the following levels of security classification: COSMIC TOP SECRET (CTS), NATO SECRET (NS), NATO CONFIDENTIAL (NC), and NATO RESTRICTED (NR). Another marking, ATOMAL, is applied to U.S. RESTRICTED DATA or FORMERLY RESTRICTED DATA and UK Atomic information that has been released to NATO. ATOMAL information is marked COSMIC TOP SECRET ATOMAL (CTSA), NATO SECRET ATOMAL (NSA), or NATO CONFIDENTIAL ATOMAL (NCA).

10-702. NATO RESTRICTED. NATO RESTRICTED does not correspond to an equivalent U.S. classification. NATO RESTRICTED does not require a PCL for access. An FCL is not required if the only information to which the company will have access is NATO RESTRICTED. IS handling only NATO RESTRICTED information do not require certification or accreditation. NATO RESTRICTED information may be included in U.S. unclassified documents. The U.S. document must be marked, "THIS DOCUMENT CONTAINS NATO RESTRICTED INFORMATION." NATO RESTRICTED material may be stored in locked filing cabinets, bookcases, desks, or other similar locked containers that will deter unauthorized access.

10-703. NATO Contracts. NATO contracts involving NATO-unique systems, programs, or operations are awarded by a NATO Production and Logistics Organization (NPLO), a designated NATO Management Agency, the NATO Research Staff, or a NATO Command. In the case of NATO infrastructure projects (e.g., airfields, communications), the NATO contract is awarded by a contracting agency or prime contractor of the NATO nation responsible for the infrastructure project.

10-704. NATO Facility Security Clearance Certificate. A NATO Facility Security Clearance Certificate (FSCC) is required for a contractor to negotiate or perform on a NATO classified contract A U.S. facility qualifies for a NATO FSCC if it has an equivalent U.S. FCL and its personnel have been briefed on NATO procedures. The CSA shall provide the NATO FSCC to the requesting activity. A NATO FSCC is not required for GCA contracts involving access to NATO classified information.

10-705. PCL Requirements. Access to NATO classified information requires a final PCL at the equivalent level.

10-706. NATO Briefings. Before having access to NATO classified information, employees shall be given a NATO security briefing that covers the requirements of this section and the consequences of negligent handling of NATO classified information. The FSO shall be initially briefed by a representative of the CSA. Annual refresher briefings shall also be conducted. When access to NATO classified information is no longer required, the employee shall be debriefed. The employee shall sign a certificate stating that they have been briefed or debriefed, as applicable, and acknowledge their responsibility for safeguarding NATO information. Certificates shall be maintained for 2 years for NATO SECRET and CONFIDENTIAL, and 3 years for COSMIC TOP SECRET and all ATOMAL information. The contractor shall maintain a record of all NATO briefings and debriefings in the CSA-designated database.

10-707. Access to NATO Classified Information by Foreign Nationals. Foreign nationals of non-NATO nations may have access to NATO classified information only with the consent of the NATO Office of Security and the contracting activity. Requests shall be submitted to the Central U.S. Registry (CUSR). Access to NATO classified information may be permitted for citizens of NATO member nations, provided a NATO security clearance certificate is provided by their government and they have been briefed.

10-708. Subcontracting for NATO Contracts. The contractor shall obtain prior written approval from the NATO contracting activity and a NATO FSCC must be issued prior to awarding the subcontract. The request for approval will be forwarded through the CSA.

10-709. Preparing and Marking NATO Documents. All classified documents created by a U.S. contractor shall be portion-marked. Any portion extracted from a NATO document that is not portion marked, must be assigned the classification that is assigned to the NATO document.

a. All U.S.-originated NATO classified documents shall bear an assigned reference number and date on the first page. The reference numbers shall be assigned as follows:

(1) The first element shall be the abbreviation for the name of the contractor facility.

(2) The second element shall be the abbreviation for the overall classification followed by a hyphen and the 4-digit sequence number for the document within that classification that has been generated for the applicable calendar year.

(3) The third element shall be the year; e.g., MM/NS-0013/93.

b. COSMIC TOP SECRET, NATO SECRET, and ATOMAL documents shall bear the reference number on each page and a copy number on the cover or first page. Copies of NATO documents shall be serially numbered. Pages shall be numbered. The first page or index or table of contents shall include a list, including page numbers, of all Annexes and Appendices. The total number of pages shall be stated on the first page. All Annexes or Appendices will include the date of the original document and the purpose of the new text (addition or substitution) on the first page.

c. One of the following markings shall be applied to NATO documents that contain ATOMAL information:

(1) "This document contains U.S. ATOMIC Information (RESTRICTED DATA or FORMERLY RESTRICTED DATA) made available pursuant to the NATO Agreement for Cooperation Regarding ATOMIC Information, dated 18 June 1964, and will be safeguarded accordingly."

(2) "This document contains UK ATOMIC Information. This information is released to NATO including its military and civilian agencies and member states on condition that it will not be released by the recipient organization to any other organization or government or national of another country or member of any other organization without prior permission from H.M. Government in the United Kingdom."

d. Working papers shall be retained only until a final product is produced.

10-710. Classification Guidance. Classification guidance shall be in the form of a NATO security aspects letter and a security requirements checklist for NATO contracts, or a Contract Security Classification Specification. If adequate classification guidance is not received, the contractor shall contact the CSA for assistance. NATO classified documents and NATO information in other documents shall not be declassified or downgraded without the prior written consent of the originating activity. Recommendations concerning the declassification or downgrading of NATO classified information shall be forwarded to the CUSR.

10-711. Further Distribution. The contractor shall not release or disclose NATO classified information to a third party or outside the contractor's facility for any purpose without the prior written approval of the contracting agency.

10-712. Storage of NATO Documents. NATO classified documents shall be stored as prescribed for U.S. documents of an equivalent classification level, except as follows:

a. NATO classified documents shall not be commingled with other documents.

b. Combinations for containers used to store NATO classified information shall be changed annually. The combination also shall be changed when an individual with access to the container departs or no longer requires access to the container, and if the combination is suspected of being compromised.

c. When the combination is recorded it shall be marked with the highest classification level of documents stored in the container as well as to indicate the level and type of NATO documents in the container. The combination record must be logged and controlled in the same manner as NATO classified documents.

10-713. International Transmission. NATO has a registry system for the receipt and distribution of NATO documents within each NATO member nation. The central distribution point for the U.S. is the CUSR located in the Pentagon. The CUSR establishes subregistries at U.S. Government organizations for further distribution and control of NATO documents. Subregistries may establish control points at contractor facilities. COSMIC TOP SECRET, NATO SECRET, and all ATOMAL documents shall be transferred through the registry system. NATO CONFIDENTIAL documents provided as part of NATO infrastructure contracts shall be transmitted via government channels in compliance with Section 4 of this Chapter.

10-714. Hand Carrying. NATO SECRET and NATO CONFIDENTIAL documents may be hand carried across international borders if authorized by the GCA. The courier shall be issued a NATO Courier Certificate by the CSA. When hand carrying is authorized, the documents shall be delivered to a U.S. organization at NATO, which shall transfer them to the intended NATO recipient.

10-715. Reproduction. Reproductions of COSMIC TOP SECRET and COSMIC TOP SECRET ATOMAL information shall be performed by the responsible Registry. The reproduction of NATO SECRET, and CONFIDENTIAL documents may be authorized to meet contractual requirements unless reproduction is prohibited by the contracting entity. Copies of COSMIC TOP SECRET, NATO SECRET, and ATOMAL documents shall be serially numbered and controlled and accounted for in the same manner as the original.

10-716. Disposition. Generally, all NATO classified documents shall be returned to the contracting activity that provided them on completion of the contract. Documents provided in connection with an invitation to bid also shall be returned immediately if the bid is not accepted or submitted. NATO classified documents may also be destroyed when permitted. COSMIC TOP SECRET and COSMIC TOP SECRET ATOMAL documents shall be destroyed by the Registry that provided the documents. Destruction certificates are required for all NATO classified documents except NATO CONFIDENTIAL. The destruction of COSMIC TOP SECRET, NATO SECRET and all ATOMAL documents must be witnessed.

10-717. Accountability Records. Logs, receipts, and destruction certificates are required for NATO classified information, as described below. Records for NATO documents shall be maintained separately from records of non-NATO documents. COSMIC TOP SECRET and all ATOMAL documents shall be recorded on logs maintained separately from other NATO logs and shall be assigned unique serial control numbers. Additionally, disclosure records bearing the name and signature of each person who has access are required for all COSMIC TOP SECRET, COSMIC TOP SECRET ATOMAL, and all other ATOMAL or NATO classified documents to which special access limitations have been applied.

a. Minimum identifying data on logs, receipts, and destruction certificates shall include the NATO reference number, short title, date of the document, classification, and serial copy numbers. Logs shall reflect the short title, unclassified subject, and distribution of the documents.

b. Receipts are required for all NATO classified documents except NATO CONFIDENTIAL.

c. Inventories shall be conducted annually of all COSMIC TOP SECRET, NATO SECRET, and all ATOMAL documents.

d. Records shall be retained for 10 years for COSMIC TOP SECRET and COSMIC TOP SECRET ATOMAL documents and 5 years for NATO SECRET, NATO SECRET ATOMAL, NATO CONFIDENTIAL, and NATO CONFIDENTIAL ATOMAL documents.

10-718. Security Violations and Loss, Compromise, or Possible Compromise. The contractor shall immediately report the loss, compromise, or suspected loss or compromise, as well as any other security violations involving NATO classified information to the CSA.

10-719. Extracting from NATO Documents. Permission to extract from a COSMIC TOP SECRET or ATOMAL document shall be obtained from the CUSR.

a. If extracts of NATO information are included in a U.S. document prepared for a non-NATO contract, the document shall be marked with U.S. classification markings. The caveat, "THIS DOCUMENT CONTAINS NATO (level of classification) INFORMATION" also shall be marked on the front cover or first page of the document. Additionally, each paragraph or portion containing the NATO information shall be marked with the appropriate NATO classification, abbreviated in parentheses (e.g., NS) preceding the portion or paragraph. The "Declassify on" line of the document shall show "Source marked OADR" and the date of origin of the most recent source document unless the original NATO document shows a specific date for declassification.

b. The declassification or downgrading of NATO information in a U.S. document requires the approval of the originating NATO activity. Requests shall be submitted to the CUSR for NATO contracts, through the GCA for U.S. contracts, and through the CSA for non-NATO contracts awarded by a NATO member nation.

10-720. Release of U.S. Information to NATO.

a. Release of U.S. classified or export-controlled information to NATO requires an export authorization or other written disclosure authorization. When a document containing U.S. classified information is being prepared for NATO, the appropriate NATO classification markings shall be applied to the document. Documents containing U.S. classified information and U.S. classified documents that are authorized for release to NATO shall be marked on the cover or first page "THIS DOCUMENT CONTAINS U.S. CLASSIFIED INFORMATION. THE INFORMATION IN THIS DOCUMENT HAS BEEN AUTHORIZED FOR RELEASE TO (cite the NATO organization) BY (cite the applicable license or other written authority)." The CSA shall provide transmission instructions to the contractor. The material shall be addressed to a U.S. organization at NATO, which shall then place the material into NATO security channels. The material shall be accompanied by a letter to the U.S. organization that provides transfer instructions and assurances that the material has been authorized for release to NATO. The inner wrapper shall be addressed to the intended NATO recipient. Material to be sent to NATO via mail shall be routed through the U.S. Postal Service and U.S. military postal channels to the U.S. organization that will make the transfer.

b. A record shall be maintained that identifies the originator and source of classified information that are used in the preparation of documents for release to NATO. The record shall be provided with any request for release authorization.

10-721. Visits. NATO visits are visits by personnel representing a NATO entity and relating to NATO contracts and programs. NATO visits shall be handled in accordance with the requirements in Section 5 of this chapter. A NATO Certificate of Security Clearance will be included with the visit request.

a. **NPLO and NATO Industrial Advisory Group (NIAG) Recurring Visits.** NATO has established special procedures for recurring visits involving contractors, government departments and agencies, and NATO commands and agencies that are participating in a NPLO or NIAG contract or program. The NATO Management Office or Agency responsible for the NPLO program will prepare a list of the Government and contractor facilities participating in the program. For NIAG programs, the list will be prepared by the responsible NATO staff element. The list will be forwarded to the appropriate clearance agency of the participating nations, which will forward it to the participating contractor.

b. **Visitor Record.** The contractor shall maintain a record of NATO visits including those by U.S. personnel assigned to NATO. The records shall be maintained for 3 years.

Section 8. Transfers of Defense Articles to AUS or the UK without a License or Other Written Authorization

10-800 General. On June 21, 2007, the U.S. signed the Defense Trade Cooperation Treaty between the Government of the United States of America and the Government of the UK of Great Britain and Northern Ireland (reference (ao)) and on September 5, 2007 between the Government of the United States of America and the Government of AUS (reference (ap)) concerning Defense Trade Cooperations (U.S.-UK Treaty and U.S.-AUS Treaty, referred to collectively in this Manual as "the Treaties"). The U.S.-UK Treaty entered into force on April 13, 2012. The U.S.-AUS Treaty entered into force on May 16, 2013. The Treaties provide a comprehensive framework for exports and transfers to the UK or AUS of certain classified and unclassified defense articles without a license or other written authorization. Reference (v) has been amended to implement the Treaties through new exemptions in parts 126.16 and 126.17. Supplement No. 1 to part 126 of reference (v) identifies those defense articles and services that are not eligible for export via Treaty exemptions. This exemption applies to contractors registered with the DDTC, and eligible to export defense articles.

10-801 Defense Articles. Defense articles fall under the scope of the Treaties when they are in support of:

    a. U.S. and UK or U.S. and AUS combined military or counter-terrorism operations;

    b. U.S. and UK or U.S. and AUS cooperative security and defense research, development, production, and support programs;

    c. Mutually agreed specific security and defense projects where the Governments of the UK or AUS is the end-user; or

    d. U.S. Government end-use.

10-802. Marking Requirements. Contractors are required to mark defense articles that fall under the scope of the treaty prior to transferring from the U.S. to the UK as follows:

a. Classified U.S. Defense Articles shall be marked:

    (1) Treaty with the Government of UK

CLASSIFICATION LEVEL USML//REL GBR AND USA TREATY COMMUNITY//

For example, for defense articles classified SECRET, the marking shall be "SECRET USML//REL GBR AND USA TREATY COMMUNITY//"

    (2) Treaty with the Government of AUS

//CLASSIFICATION LEVEL USML//REL AUS AND USA TREATY COMMUNITY//

For example, for Defense Articles classified SECRET, the marking will be "//SECRET USML//REL AUS AND USA TREATY COMMUNITY//"

    b. All other standard classification markings in accordance with Chapter 4, Section 2 of this Manual shall apply.

    c. Unclassified U.S. defense articles shall be marked:

    (1) Treaty with the Government of UK

//RESTRICTED USML//REL GBR AND USA TREATY COMMUNITY//

    (2) Treaty with the Government of AUS

//RESTRICTED USML//REL AUS AND USA TREATY COMMUNITY//

    d. When defense articles are returned from the UK or AUS to the U.S., any defense articles marked as RESTRICTED in this manner purely for the purposes of the Treaties shall be considered to be unclassified and such marking shall be removed.

10-803. Notice. The following notice shall be included (e.g., as part of the bill of lading) whenever defense articles are exported in accordance with the provisions of these Treaties and reference (v):

These U.S. Munitions List commodities are authorized by the U.S. Government under the U.S.-[AUS or UK, as applicable] Defense Trade Cooperation Treaty for export only to [AUS or UK, as applicable] for use in approved projects, programs or operations by members of the [AUS or UK, as applicable] Community. They may not be retransferred or re-exported or used outside of an approved project, program, or operation, either in their original form or after being incorporated into other end-items, without the prior written approval of the U.S. Department of State.

10-804. Labelling

a. Defense articles (as defined in section 120.6 of reference (v)) (other than technical data) will be individually labeled with the appropriate identification; or, where such labeling is impracticable (e.g., propellants, chemicals), will be accompanied by documentation (such as contracts or invoices) clearly associating the defense articles with the appropriate markings.

b. Technical data (as defined in section 120.10 of reference (v)) (including data packages, technical papers, manuals, presentations, specifications, guides and reports), regardless of media or means of transmission (i.e., physical, oral, or electronic), will be individually labeled with the appropriate identification detailed; or, where such labeling is impracticable will be accompanied by documentation (such as contracts or invoices) or oral notification clearly associating the technical data with the appropriate markings.

c. Defense services (as defined in section 120.9 of reference (v)) will be accompanied by documentation (contracts, invoices, shipping bills, or bills of lading) clearly labeled with the appropriate identification.

10-805. Transfers.

a. All Defense Articles that fall under the scope of the Treaties must be transferred from the U.S. point of embarkation through channels approved by both the U.S. and the UK or the U.S. and AUS, as applicable.

b. For transfers of defense articles as freight, the contractor shall prepare a transportation plan. For transfer of classified U.S. defense articles, a freight forwarder must have a valid facility security clearance (FCL) and storage capability at the appropriate level. For unclassified U.S. defense articles that are transferred as freight, a freight forwarder is not required to be cleared.

10-806 Records. Contractors shall maintain records of exports, transfers, re-exports, or re-transfers of defense articles subject to the Treaties for a minimum of 5 years. Records shall be made available to DSS upon request. The records shall contain the following information required by Sections 126.16 and 126.17 of reference (v):

a. Port of entry or exit.

b. Date and time of export or import.

c. Method of export or import.

d. Commodity code and description of the commodity, including technical data.

e. Value of export.

f. Justification for export under the Treaties.

g. End-user or end-use.

h. Identification of all U.S. and foreign parties to the transaction.

i. How export was marked.

j. Security classification of the export.

k. All written correspondence with the U.S. Government on the export.

l. All information relating to political contributions, fees, or commissions furnished or obtained, offered, solicited, or agreed upon, as outlined in parts 126.16(m) or 126.17(m) of reference (v).

m. Purchase order, contract, or letter of intent.

n. Technical data actually exported.

o. The Internal Transaction Number for the Electronic Export Information filing in the Automated Export System.

p. All shipping documentation (including, but not limited to, the airway bill, bill of lading, packing list, delivery verification, and invoice).

q. Statement of Registration (Form DS-2032).

CHAPTER 11
Miscellaneous Information

Section 1. TEMPEST

11-100. General. TEMPEST is an unclassified short name referring to investigations and studies of compromising emanations. Compromising emanations are unintentional intelligence-bearing signals that, if intercepted and analyzed, will disclose classified information when it is transmitted, received, handled, or otherwise processed by any information processing equipment.

11-101. TEMPEST Requirements.

a. TEMPEST countermeasures will be applied only in proportion to the threat of exploitation and the resulting damage to the national security should the information be intercepted and analyzed by a foreign intelligence organization. It is the responsibility of the GCA to identify in writing what TEMPEST countermeasures may be required. The GCA will identify any TEMPEST requirements within the United States to the CSA for approval prior to imposing requirements for TEMPEST countermeasures on contractors. Contractors may not impose TEMPEST countermeasures upon their subcontractors without GCA and CSA approval.

b. The government is responsible for performing threat assessment and vulnerability studies when it is determined that classified information may be exposed to TEMPEST collection.

c. Contractors will assist the GCA in conducting threat and vulnerability surveys by providing the following information upon request:

(1) The specific classification and special categories of material to be processed/handled by electronic means.

(2) The specific location where classified processing will be performed.

(3) The name, address, title, and contact information for a point-of-contact at the facility where processing will occur.

11-102. Cost. All costs associated with applying TEMPEST countermeasures, when such countermeasures are imposed upon the contractor by a GCA, shall be recoverable by direct charge to the applicable contract. The GCA should provide TEMPEST shielding and shielded equipment as government-furnished equipment (GFE) when such extreme countermeasures are deemed essential to the protection of the information being processed.

Section 2. Defense Technical Information Center (DTIC)

11-200. General. The Department of Defense operates certain activities to assist individuals and organizations in gaining access to scientific and technical information describing planned or on-going research, development, test, and evaluation (RDT&E) efforts of the Department of Defense. DTIC is the central point within the Department of Defense for acquiring, storing, retrieving, and disseminating scientific and technical information to support the management and conduct of DoD RDT&E and study programs.

11-201. User Community. DTIC services are available to the Department of Defense and its contractors, as well as to other U.S. Government organizations and their contractors. Contractors may also become eligible for services under the Defense Potential Contractors Program.

11-202. Registration Process. All users are required to register for service. Registration, which is free, generally involves completing two forms which are available from DTIC as part of a registration kit.

a. DD Form 1540, Registration for Scientific and Technical Information Services. This form shall be completed for each contract that authorizes use of DTIC services. This authorization is included in the Contract Security Classification Specification. The DD Form 1540 is submitted to DTIC through the sponsoring GCA for certification and approval. If a subcontract is involved, the DD Form 1540 is submitted through the prime contractor. The DD Form 1540 remains in force until completion of the classified contract or subcontract.

b. DD Form 2345, Militarily Critical Technical Data Agreement. Qualified contractors are eligible for access to militarily critical technical data after certification with Defense Logistics Services Center (DLSC) by completing the DD Form 2345. This DLSC certification is supplementary to registration with the DTIC. Upon certification with DLSC, the user also may be eligible for access to unclassified, militarily critical technical data from other DoD sources.

11-203. Safeguarding Requirements. Classified information acquired from DTIC shall be safeguarded according to the requirements of this Manual and with any restrictions that are marked on the material itself. The specific contract number that authorized contractor access to the information shall be placed on each classified document. When the contract to which the DD Form 1540 applies is completed or terminated, the contractor shall either destroy or request retention for the material.

11-204. DTIC Downgrading or Declassification Notices. DTIC re-marks downgraded or declassified paper documents only on the front and back covers and the title, first, and back pages. It is the responsibility of the recipient to complete any remarking required. Documents originally marked under the provisions of previous E.O.s may contain pages that do not bear any classification markings. Before extracting or reproducing the information from these pages, contractors should direct any questions they may have to the originator of the document.

11-205. Questions Concerning Reference Material. Most material made available to contractors by DTIC and other distribution agencies is reference material. Therefore, the GCA that authorized the services of DTIC under a specific contract may not be in a position to provide the contractor with classification guidance for the reference material. Classification jurisdiction always is the responsibility of the originating agency, or its successor. Classification jurisdiction is not necessarily the responsibility of the authorizing GCA. When a contractor needs assistance in identifying the responsible department or agency for classification guidance for reference material the CSA should be consulted.

11-206. Subcontracts. If a contractor awards a subcontract that authorizes the subcontractor to use the services of DTIC and is expected to require access only to classified reference material, the Contract Security Classification Specification issued to the subcontractor shall show the highest category of classification required. The Contract Security Classification Specification will have a statement similar to the following: "Information extracted from classified reference material shall be classified according to the markings on such material. The DD Form 1540 prepared under this subcontract shall be forwarded through (name of prime contractor)."

Section 3. Independent Research and Development (IR&D) Efforts

11-300. General. This section provides special procedures and requirements necessary for safeguarding classified information when it is incorporated in contractors' IR&D efforts.

11-301. Information Generated Under an IR&D Effort that Incorporates Classified Information. Under reference (b) information that is in substance the same as information currently classified requires a derivative classification. Therefore, information in a contractor's IR&D effort will require a derivative classification.

11-302. Classification Guidance. The releasing contractor may extract guidance appropriate for the IR&D effort from:

    a. An existing Contract Security Classification Specification that was previously furnished by a GCA in connection with performance of a classified contract;

    b. A final Contract Security Classification Specification that was issued in connection with retention of classified documents under a completed contract;

    c. A security classification guide obtained from DTIC; or

    d. A classified source document.

NOTE: The Department of Defense "Index of Security Classification Guides" and many of the listed security classification guides are available to contractors who are registered with the DTIC. Contractors are encouraged to use the Index and the listed guides to obtain up-to-date security guidance for the classified information involved when developing guidance appropriate for their IR&D efforts.

11-303. Preparation of Security Guidance. Contractors shall use the Contract Security Classification Specification to provide security guidance for the classified information released in their IR&D efforts.

11-304. Retention of Classified Documents Generated Under IR&D Efforts. Contractors may retain the classified documents that were generated in connection with their classified IR&D efforts for the duration of their FCL provided they have proper storage capability. Documents shall be clearly identified as "IR&D DOCUMENTS." A contractor's facility clearance will not be continued solely for the purpose of retention of classified IR&D documents without specific retention authorization from the GCA that has jurisdiction over the classified information contained in such documents. Contractors shall establish procedures for review of their IR&D documents on a recurring basis to reduce their classified inventory to the minimum necessary.

APPENDIX A

Cognizant Security Office Information

DoD

DoD as a CSA, designates DSS as its CSO. DSS is headquartered in Northern Virginia. The field organization structure consists of four regions. Each region is comprised of Field Offices that employ Industrial Security Representatives (ISRs) to provide security oversight, consultation and assistance to over 13,000 contractors. The DSS Field Offices and the ISRs have supporting IS Security Professionals and Counterintelligence personnel, who work with the contractor on NISPOM-related matters. Field offices are located throughout the United States. Refer to the DSS website (www.dss.mil) for a listing of office locations and areas of responsibility.

Verification of Facility Clearance and Safeguarding: www.dss.mil

Other questions: DoD Security Services Center
Phone: 1-888-282-7682

DOE

DOE, as a CSA, designates the DOE Field Office Safeguards and Security Divisions as its CSO, Clearance Agency, CVA, Adjudicative Authority, and PCL and FCL databases for its contractors.

Office of Headquarters Security Operations
SO-30/Germantown Building
U.S. Department of Energy
1000 Independence Avenue, S.W.
Washington, D.C. 20585-1290
(301) 903-4175

U.S. Department of Energy
National Nuclear Security Administration Office of Personnel and Facility Clearances
Pennsylvania & H Street, Kirtland Air Force Base
Albuquerque, NM 87116
(505) 845- 4844

U.S. Department of Energy
Chicago Office, Bldg. 201
9800 South Cass Avenue
Argonne, IL 60439
(630) 252-2000 (Operator)

U.S. Department of Energy
Idaho Operations Office
850 Energy Drive
Idaho Falls, ID 83401
(208) 526-1322

U.S. Department of Energy
Oak Ridge Operations Office
200 Administration Road
Oak Ridge, TN 37831
(865) 576-2140

U.S. Department of Energy
Pittsburgh Naval Reactors
814 Pittsburgh McKeesport Boulevard
West Mifflin, PA 15122-0109
(412) 476-5000

U.S. Department of Energy
Richland Operations Office
825 Jadwin Avenue
P.O. Box 550
Richland, WA 99352
(509) 376-7411

U.S. Department of Energy
Savannah River Operations Office
Road 1A
Aiken, SC 29801
(803) 725-6211

U.S. Department of Energy
Schenectady Naval Reactors Office
U.S. DOE Building MS Warehouse
2401 River Road
Schenectady, NY 12309
(518) 395-4000

For International Affairs and Industrial Security International, the DOE designates the:

Office of International Safeguards and Security
SO-20.3/Germantown Building
U.S. Department of Energy
1000 Independence Avenue, S.W.
Washington, D.C. 20585-1290
(301) 903-2910

Nuclear Regulatory Commission

The NRC, as a CSA, designates the following office as its CSO, Adjudicative Authority, International Affairs Office, PCL and FCL databases, and the Office of Industrial Security International for their contractors.

U.S. Nuclear Regulatory Commission
ATTN: Director of Security
Washington, DC 20555
(301) 415-8100

The NRC designates the following offices as the Clearance Agency and Central Verification Agency for its contractors.

Clearance Agency:
U.S. Nuclear Regulatory Commission
ATTN: Director of Security Personnel Security Branch
Washington D.C. 20555
(301) 415-7043

Central Verification Agency:
U.S. Nuclear Regulatory Commission
ATTN: Director of Security Facilities Security Branch
Washington, D.C. 20555
(301) 415-7407

APPENDIX B

International Visits
Standard Request for Visit Format (RFV)

This appendix contains the instructions for the completion of a Request for Visit (RFV) for international visits. The visit request must be submitted through the FSO to the applicable clearance agency. The RFV format below, will be used for all requests for international visits as follows:

(1) A separate request must be submitted for each program, project, or contract.

(2) A separate request must be submitted for each country to be visited.

(3) Subject to Government Agency restrictions, multiple locations may be listed for each country provided each location is involved in the same program, project, or contract.

(4) The RFV may be locally produced on a form or form letter provided the specified format is followed. Information given to answer each data element must be typed or printed in block letters so that it is legible.

1. GENERAL INSTRUCTION

1.1. The RFV is an important document and must be completed without misstatement or omission. Failure to provide all requested information will delay the processing of the request.

1.2. The RFV should be used for a "one-time visit" and/or "recurring visits" and/or an "emergency visit" during a certain period of time not to exceed one year.

1.3. The RFV should be marked to identify which type of information or subject will be involved:

1.3.1. Unclassified/RESTRICTED information without access to information or areas classified CONFIDENTIAL or above.

1.3.2. Information or areas classified CONFIDENTIAL or above.

1.4. This RFV should be hand written in block letters or typed. Processing of the RFV in an IS is allowed provided that the original form and content are consistent.

1.5. **Submitting Terms and Country Codes.**

The RFV should be in the possession of the requesting National Security Authority/Designated Security Authority (NSA/DSA) the number of working days prior to the visit as follows:

Country to be visited	2 letter-code	Working days (if different from lead times as shown in Section I)
Austria	AT	20
Belgium	BE	20
Canada	CA	20
Czech Republic	CZ	20
Denmark	DA	7
France	FR	15
Germany	GE	20
Greece	GR	20
Hungary	HU	20
Italy	IT	20
Luxembourg	LU	14
Netherlands	NL	10
Norway	NO	10
Portugal	PO	21
Poland	PL	25
Spain	SP	20
Sweden	SE	15
Switzerland	SZ	20
Turkey	TU	21
United Kingdom	UK	15
United States	US	21

1.6. The completed RFV should be sent to the following national agency/address that will process the request (to be inserted by issuing NSA/DSA):

Name of Agency	
Address:	
Telefax no:	

DETAILED INSTRUCTIONS FOR COMPLETION OF REQUEST FOR VISIT
(The application has to be submitted in English only)

These detailed instructions are guidance for the visitors who complete the RFV in the case of one-time visits or by the agency or facility security officer in case of recurring visits in the framework of approved programs or projects. Since this RFV-format is designed for manual as well as for automated use it is required that a corresponding distinction is made in the completion of some items. When this distinction is applicable reference is made in the text of the item under "Remark(s)".

Heading: In case of a <u>manual</u> application mark the appropriate box in left, <u>middle</u> and right column.

HEADING	Check boxes for visit type, information or access type, and whether or not there are annexes to the RFV.
1. ADMINISTRATIVE DATA	Do not fill in (to be completed by requesting Embassy).
2. REQUESTING GOVERNMENT AGENCY OR INDUSTRIAL FACILITY.	Mention full name and postal address. Include city, state, postal zone as applicable.
3. GOVERNMENT AGENCY OR INDUSTRIAL FACILITY TO BE VISITED	Mention full name and postal address. Include city, state, postal zone, telex or fax number, telephone number and e-mail. Mention the name and telephone/fax numbers and e-mail of your main point of contact or the person with whom you have made the appointment for the visit. Remarks: 1) Mentioning the correct postal zone (zip code) is very important because there can be different facilities of the same company. 2) In case of a manual application, Annex 1 can be used when two or more agencies or facilities have to be visited in the framework of the same subject. When an Annex is used item 3 should state: "SEE ANNEX 1, NUMBER OF AGENCIES/FAC.:.." (state number of agencies/ facilities). 3) For visits to the United States one request for each agency/facility to be visited should be filled in.
4. DATES OF VISIT	Mention the actual date or period (date-to-date) of the visit by "day- month-year". If applicable, place an alternate date or period in brackets.
5. TYPE OF VISIT	Mark one item of each column as indicated. Government initiative will be specified only if the visit is in support of an authorized government program, which must be fully described in item 8.

6. **SUBJECT TO BE DISCUSSED/ JUSTIFICATION**	Give a brief description of the subject(s) motivating the visit. Do not use unexplained abbreviations. <u>Remarks:</u> 1) In case of a recurring visit this item should state "Recurring Visits" as the first words in the data element (e.g. Recurring Visits to discuss_____) 2) It is strongly advised to repeat the subject to be discussed and or the justification of the visit in the language of the receiving country.
7. **ANTICIPATED LEVEL OF CLASSIFIED INFORMATION TO BE INVOLVED**	TOP SECRET (TS) SECRET (S) CONFIDENTIAL (C) RESTRICTED (R) UNCLASSIFIED (U)– As applicable
8. **IS THE VISIT PERTINENT TO:** Specific equipment or weapon system Foreign military sales or export license A Program or Agreement A defense acquisition process Other	Mark the appropriate line yes (Y) and specify the full name of the government project/program, FMS-case etc., or request for proposal or tender offer using commonly used abbreviations only

9. **PARTICULARS OF VISITOR**	<u>NAME:</u> Title (Mr. Dr. COL), family name, first forename in full, middle initial(s), and suffix (Jr., PhD, etc.) Family name and first forename are mandatory fields.
	<u>DOB:</u> date of birth (day-month-year)
	<u>POB:</u> place of birth (city-state-country)
	<u>SC:</u> actual security clearance status, e.g., TS, S, C. Indicate NATO clearance (CTS, NS, NC) if the visit is related to NATO business.
	<u>ID-PP:</u> enter the number of identification card or passport, as required by host government.
	<u>NAT:</u> enter nationality and/or citizenship in 2-letter-code in accordance with the General Instructions paragraph 1.4.
	<u>POSITION:</u> Mention the position the visitor holds in the organization (e.g., director, product manager, etc.)
	<u>COMPANY/AGENCY:</u> Mention the name of the government agency or industrial facility that the visitor represents (if different from item 2).
	[Remark: when more than 2 visitors are involved in the visit, Annex 2 should be used. In that case item no. 9 should state "SEE ANNEX 2, NUMBER OF VISITORS:" (state the number of visitors)].
10. **THE SECURITY OFFICER OF THE REQUESTING AGENCY**	This items requires the name, telephone, facsimile numbers and e-mail of the requesting facility security officer

11. CERTIFICATION OF SECURITY CLEARANCE	DO NOT FILL IN (to be completed by government certifying authority only if access to information or to areas classified CONFIDENTIAL or above will be involved unless otherwise required by bilateral agreements.) Note for the certifying authority: a. Mention name, address, telephone, facsimile numbers and e-mail (can be pre-printed). b. This item should be signed and eventually stamped, as applicable. c. If the certifying authority corresponds with the requesting National Security Authority enter: "See item 12". Remark: Item 11 and 12 may be filled in by the appropriate official of the Embassy of the requesting country.
12. REQUESTING SECURITY AUTHORITY	DO NOT FILL IN. Note for the requesting NSA/DSA: a. Mention name, address, telephone, facsimile numbers and e-mail (can be pre-printed). b. Sign and eventually stamp this item.
13. REMARKS	a. This item can be used for certain administrative requirements (e.g. proposed itinerary, request for hotel, and/or transportation). b. This space is also available for the receiving NSA/DSA for processing, e.g., "no security objections", etc. c. In case of an Emergency Visit the name, telephone, fax numbers and e-mail of the knowledgeable person (Doc. 7, section II, point 2a) should be stated. d. In case a special briefing is required, the type of briefing and the date that the briefing was given should be stated.

REQUEST FOR VISIT		
[ ] One-time [ ] Recurring [ ] Emergency [ ] Amendment	[ ] Unclassified/RESTRICTED information or access to areas without access to information classified CONFIDENTIAL or above [ ] CONFIDENTIAL or above involved.	Annexes: [ ] Yes [ ] No

1. ADMINISTRATIVE DATA

REQUESTOR: TO:	DATE: VISIT ID:

2. REQUESTING GOVERNMENT AGENCY OR INDUSTRIAL FACILITY

NAME POSTAL ADDRESS	E-MAIL ADDRESS (when known)
TELEX/FAX NR.	TELEPHONE

3. GOVERNMENT AGENCY OR INDUSTRIAL FACILITY TO BE VISITED

NAME	
ADDRESS	E-MAIL ADDRESS (when known)
TELEX/FAX NR.	TELEPHONE
POINT OF CONTACT	

4. DATES OF VISIT: / / TO / / (/ / TO / /)

5 TYPE OF VISIT: (SELECT ONE FROM EACH COLUMN)

[ ] GOVERNMENT INTITIATIVE	[ ] INITIATED BY REQUESTING AGENCY OR FACILITY
[ ] COMMERCIAL INITIATIVE	[ ] BY INVITIATION OF THE FACILITY TO BE VISITED

6. SUBJECT TO BE DISCUSSED/JUSTIFICATION:

7. ANTICIPATED LEVEL OF CLASSIFIED INFORMATION TO BE INVOLVED

8. IS THE VISIT PERTINENT TO:		*SPECIFY*
Specific equipment or weapon system	[ ]	
Foreign military sales or export license	[ ]	
A Program or Agreement	[ ]	
A defence acquisition process	[ ]	
Other	[ ]	

9. PARTICULARS OF VISITORS

NAME	
DATE OF BIRTH; / /	PLACE OF BIRTH
SECURITY CLEARANCE:	ID/PP NR:
POSITION	NATIONALITY
COMPANY/AGENCY	

NAME	
DATE OF BIRTH; / /	PLACE OF BIRTH
SECURITY CLEARANCE:	ID/PP NR:
POSITION	NATIONALITY
COMPANY/AGENCY	

10. THE SECURITY OFFICER OF THE REQUESTING GOVERNMENT AGENCY OR INDUSTRIAL FACILITY

NAME:	TELEPHONE/FAX NRS. E-MAIL-ADDRESS (when known):
SIGNATURE:	

11. CERTIFICATON OF SECURITY CLEARANCE
(only if information or areas classified CONFIDENTIAL or above will be involved unless required by bilateral agreements)

NAME:

ADDRESS:		STAMP
SIGNATURE:		

12. REQUESTING NATIONAL SECURITY AUTHORITY:

NAME:		
ADDRESS:		STAMP
SIGNATURE:		

13. REMARKS:

GOVERNMENT AGENCY OR INDUSTRIAL FACILITY TO BE VISITED:

1. NAME :   ADDRESS :

    TELEX/FAX NO :   E-MAIL (when known):
    POINT OF CONTACT :   TELEPHONE NO:

2. NAME :   ADDRESS :

    TELEX/FAX NO :   E-MAIL (when known):
    POINT OF CONTACT :   TELEPHONE NO:

3. NAME :   ADDRESS :

    TELEX/FAX NO :   E-MAIL (when known):
    POINT OF CONTACT :   TELEPHONE NO:

4. NAME :   ADDRESS :

    TELEX/FAX NO :   E-MAIL (when known):
    POINT OF CONTACT :   TELEPHONE NO:

5. NAME :   ADDRESS :

    TELEX/FAX NO :   E-MAIL (when known):
    POINT OF CONTACT :   TELEPHONE NO:

(Continue as Required)

APPENDIX C

Definitions

Unless otherwise noted, these terms and their definitions are for the purposes of this Manual.

Access. The ability and opportunity to gain knowledge of classified information.

Adverse Information. Any information that adversely reflects on the integrity or character of a cleared employee, that suggests that his or her ability to safeguard classified information may be impaired, that his or her access to classified information clearly may not be in the interest of national security, or that the individual constitutes an insider threat.

Affiliate. Any entity effectively owned or controlled by another entity.

Approved Access Control Device. An access control device that meets the requirements of this Manual as approved by the FSO.

Approved Built-in Combination Lock. A combination lock, equipped with a top-reading dial that conforms to UL Standard Number UL 768 Group 1R.

Approved Combination Padlock. A three-position dial-type changeable combination padlock listed on the GSA Qualified Products List as meeting the requirements of Federal Specification FF-P-110.

Approved Electronic, Mechanical, or Electro-Mechanical Device. An electronic, mechanical, or electro-mechanical device that meets the requirements of this *Ma*nual as approved by the FSO.

Approved Key-Operated Padlock. A padlock, which meets the requirements of MIL-SPEC-P-43607 (shrouded shackle), National Stock Number 5340-00-799-8248, or MIL-SPEC-P-43951 (regular shackle), National Stock Number 5340-00-799-8016.

Approved Security Container. A security file container, originally procured from a Federal Supply Schedule supplier that conforms to federal specifications and bears a "Test Certification Label" on the locking drawer attesting to the security capabilities of the container and lock. Such containers will be labeled "General Services Administration Approved Security Container" on the face of the top drawer. Acceptable tests of these containers can be performed only by a testing facility specifically approved by GSA.

Approved Vault. A vault constructed in accordance with this Manual and approved by the CSA.

Approved Vault Door. A vault door and frame unit originally procured from the Federal Supply Schedule (FSC Group 71, Part III, Section E, FSC Class 7110), that meets Federal Specification AA-D-600.

AUS Community. Consists of the Government of Australia entities and Australian non-governmental facilities identified on the DDTC website (http://pmddtc.state.gov/) at the time of export or transfer.

Authorized Person. A person who has a need-to-know for classified information in the performance of official duties and who has been granted a PCL at the required level.

Certification. Defined in the Committee on National Security Systems Instruction No. 4009 (reference (aq)).

Classified Contract. Any contract requiring access to classified information by a contractor or his or her employees in the performance of the contract. (A contract may be a classified contract even though the contract document is not classified.) The requirements prescribed for a "classified contract" also are applicable to all phases of precontract activity, including solicitations (bids, quotations, and proposals), precontract negotiations, post-contract activity, or other GCA program or project which requires access to classified information by a contractor.

Classification Guide. A document issued by an authorized original classifier that identifies the elements of information regarding a specific subject that must be classified and prescribes the level and duration of classification and appropriate declassification instructions. (Classification guides are provided to contractors by the Contract Security Classification Specification.)

Classified Information. Official information that has been determined, pursuant to reference (b) or any predecessor order, to require protection against unauthorized disclosure in the interest of national security and which has been so designated. The term includes NSI, RD, and FRD.

Classified Information Procedures Act. A law that provides a mechanism for the courts to determine what classified information defense counsel may access.

Classified Visit. A visit during which a visitor will require, or is expected to require, access to classified information.

Classifier. Any person who makes a classification determination and applies a classification category to information or material. The determination may be an original classification action or it may be a derivative classification action. Contractors make derivative classification determinations based on classified source material, a security classification guide, or a Contract Security Classification Specification.

Cleared Commercial Carrier. A carrier authorized by law, regulatory body, or regulation to transport SECRET material and has been granted a SECRET facility clearance.

Cleared Employees. All contractor employees granted PCLs and all employees being processed for PCLs.

Closed Area. An area that meets the requirements of this Manual for safeguarding classified material that, because of its size, nature, or operational necessity, cannot be adequately protected by the normal safeguards or stored during nonworking hours in approved containers.

Cognizant Security Agency (CSA). Agencies of the Executive Branch that have been authorized by reference (a) to establish an industrial security program to safeguard classified information under the jurisdiction of those agencies when disclosed or released to U.S. Industry. These agencies are: The Department of Defense, DOE, CIA, and NRC.

Cognizant Security Office (CSO). The organizational entity delegated by the Head of a CSA

to administer industrial security on behalf of the CSA.

Colleges and Universities. Educational institutions that award academic degrees, and related research activities directly associated with a college or university through organization or by articles of incorporation.

Communications Security (COMSEC). Protective measures taken to deny unauthorized persons information derived from telecommunications of the U.S. Government relating to national security and to ensure the authenticity of such communications.

Company. A generic and comprehensive term which may include sole proprietorships, individuals, partnerships, corporations, societies, associations, and organizations usually established and operating to carry out a commercial, industrial or other legitimate business, enterprise, or undertaking.

Compromise. An unauthorized disclosure of classified information.

CONFIDENTIAL. The classification level applied to information, the unauthorized disclosure of which reasonable could be expected to cause damage to the national security that the original classification authority is able to identify or describe.

Consignee. A person, firm, or government activity named as the receiver of a shipment; one to whom a shipment is consigned.

Consignor. A person, firm, or government activity by which articles are shipped. The consignor is usually the shipper.

Constant Surveillance Service. A transportation protective service provided by a commercial carrier qualified by SDDC to transport CONFIDENTIAL shipments. The service requires constant surveillance of the shipment at all times by a qualified carrier representative; however, an FCL is not required for the carrier. The carrier providing the service must maintain a signature and tally record for the shipment.

Contracting Officer. A government official who, in accordance with departmental or agency procedures, has the authority to enter into and administer contracts and make determinations and findings with respect thereto, or any part of such authority. The term also includes the designated representative of the contracting officer acting within the limits of his or her authority.

Contractor. Any industrial, educational, commercial, or other entity that has been granted an FCL by a CSA.

Courier. A cleared employee, designated by the contractor, whose principal duty is to transmit classified material to its destination. The classified material remains in the personal possession of the courier except for authorized overnight storage.

Corporate Family. The corporation, its subsidiaries, divisions and branch offices.

Counterintelligence. Defined in reference (e)
.

Covered IS. An IS that is owned or operated by or for a cleared defense contractor and that processes, stores, or transmits information created by or for the Department of Defense with respect to which such contractor is required to apply enhanced protection (e.g., classified information).

Custodian. An individual who has possession of, or is otherwise charged with, the responsibility for safeguarding classified information.

Cybersecurity. Defined in the National Security Presidential Directive-54 (reference (ar)). Prevention of damage to, protection of, and restoration of computers, electronic communications systems, electronic communication services, wire communication, and electronic communication, including information contained therein, to ensure its availability, integrity, authentication, confidentiality, and non-repudiation.

Cyber Incident. Actions taken through the use of computer networks that result in an actual or potentially adverse effect on an IS or the information residing therein.

Declassification. The determination that classified information no longer requires, in the interest of national security, any degree of protection against unauthorized disclosure, together with removal or cancellation of the classification designation.

Defense Articles. Those articles, services, and related technical data, including software, in tangible or intangible form, which are listed on the United States Munitions List (USML) of reference (v), as modified or amended. Defense articles exempt from

the scope of section 126.17 of reference (v) are identified in Supplement No. 1 to Part 126 of reference (v).

Derivative Classification. The incorporating, paraphrasing, restating, or generating in new form information that is already classified, and marking the newly developed material consistent with the classification markings that apply to the source information. Derivative classification includes the classification of information based on classification guidance. The duplication or reproduction of existing classified information is not derivative classification. Persons who apply derivative classification markings shall observe and respect original classification decisions and carry forward to any newly created documents any assigned authorized markings.

Document. Any recorded information, regardless of the nature of the medium or the method or circumstances of recording.

Downgrade. A determination that classified information requires, in the interest of national security, a lower degree of protection against unauthorized disclosure than currently provided, together with a changing of the classification designation to reflect a lower degree of protection.

Embedded System. An IS that performs or controls a function, either in whole or in part, as an integral element of a larger system or subsystem such as, ground support equipment, flight simulators, engine test stands, or fire control systems.

Escort. A cleared person, designated by the contractor, who accompanies a shipment of classified material to its destination. The classified material does not remain in the personal possession of the escort but the conveyance in which the material is transported remains under the constant observation and control of the escort.

Facility. A plant, laboratory, office, college, university, or commercial structure with associated warehouses, storage areas, utilities, and components, that, when related by function and location, form an operating entity. (A business or educational organization may consist of one or more facilities as defined herein.) For purposes of industrial security, the term does not include Government installations.

Facility (Security) Clearance (FCL). An administrative determination that, from a security viewpoint, a company is eligible for access to classified information of a certain category (and all lower categories).

Foreign Government Information (FGI). Information that is:

a. Provided to the U.S. by a foreign government or governments, an international organization of governments, or any element thereof with the expectation, expressed or implied, that the information, the source of the information, or both, are to be held in confidence; or

b. Produced by the U.S. pursuant to, or as a result of, a joint arrangement with a foreign government or governments, an international organization of governments, or any element thereof, requiring that the information, the arrangement, or both are to be held in confidence.

Foreign Interest. Any foreign government, agency of a foreign government, or representative of a foreign government; any form of business enterprise or legal entity organized, chartered or incorporated under the laws of any country other than the United States or its territories, and any person who is not a citizen or national of the United States.

Foreign National. Any person who is not a citizen or national of the United States.

Formerly Restricted Data (FRD). Information that has been removed from the RD category after DOE and the Department of Defense have jointly determined that the information: (1) relates primarily to the military utilization of nuclear weapons and (2) can be adequately safeguarded as NSI in the United States.

Freight Forwarder (Transportation Agent). Any agent or facility designated to receive, process, and transship U.S. material to foreign recipients. In the context of this Manual, an agent or facility cleared specifically to perform these functions for the transfer of U.S. classified material to foreign recipients.

Government Contracting Activity (GCA). An element of an agency designated by the agency head and delegated broad authority regarding acquisition functions.

Hand Carrier. A cleared employee, designated by the contractor, who occasionally hand carries classified material to its destination in connection with a classified visit or meeting. The classified material remains in the personal possession of the hand carrier except for authorized overnight storage.

Home Office Facility (HOF). The headquarters company of a multiple facility organization.

Industrial Security. That portion of information security concerned with the protection of classified information in the custody of U.S. industry.

Information. Any knowledge that can be communicated or documentary material, regardless of its physical form or characteristics.

Information Security. The result of any system of administrative policies and procedures for identifying, controlling, and protecting from unauthorized disclosure, information the protection of which is authorized by executive order.

Information System (IS). An assembly of computer hardware, software, and firmware configured for the purpose of automating the functions of calculating, computing, sequencing, storing, retrieving, displaying, communicating, or otherwise manipulating data, information and textual material.

Insider. Cleared contractor personnel with authorized access to any Government or contractor resource, including personnel, facilities, information, equipment, networks, and systems.

Insider Threat. The likelihood, risk, or potential that an insider will use his or her authorized access, wittingly or unwittingly, to do harm to the national security of the United States. Insider threats may include harm to contractor or program information, to the extent that the information impacts the contractor or agency's obligations to protect classified national security information.

Intelligence. The product resulting from the collection, evaluation, analysis, integration, and interpretation of all available information, that concerns one or more aspects of foreign nations or of areas of foreign operations, and that is immediately or potentially significant to military planning and operations.

Limited Access Authorization (LAA). Security access authorization to CONFIDENTIAL or SECRET information granted to non-U.S. citizens requiring such limited access in the course of their regular duties.

Material. Any product or substance on or in which information is embodied.

Media. Defined in reference (aq).

Multiple Facility Organization (MFO). A legal entity (single proprietorship, partnership, association, trust, or corporation) composed of two or more contractors.

National of the United States. A citizen of the United States or a person who, though not a citizen of the United States, owes permanent allegiance to the United States.

NOTE: 8 USC 1101(a)(22) (reference (x)) *lists categories of persons born in and outside the United States or its possessions who may qualify as nationals of the United States. This subsection should be consulted when doubt exists as to whether or not a person can qualify as a national of the United States.*

NATO Information. Information bearing NATO markings, indicating the information is the property of NATO, access to which is limited to representatives of NATO and its member nations unless NATO authority has been obtained to release outside of NATO.

Need-to-Know. A determination made by an authorized holder of classified information that a prospective recipient has a requirement for access to, knowledge, or possession of the classified information to perform tasks or services essential to the fulfillment of a classified contract or program.

Network. A system of two or more IS that can exchange data or information.

Original Classification. An initial determination that information requires, in the interest of national security, protection against unauthorized disclosure, together with a classification designation signifying the level of protection required. (Only government officials who have been designated in writing may apply an original classification to information.)

Parent Corporation. A corporation that owns at least a majority of another corporation's voting securities.

Personnel (Security) Clearance (PCL). An administrative determination that an individual is eligible, from a security point of view, for access to

classified information of the same or lower category as the level of the personnel clearance being granted.

Prime Contract. A contract let by a GCA to a contractor for a legitimate government purpose.

Prime Contractor. The contractor who receives a prime contract from a GCA.

Proscribed Information.

    a. Top Secret information;

    b. COMSEC information or material, excluding controlled cryptographic items when unkeyed or utilized with unclassified keys;

    c. RD as defined in reference (c);

    d. SAP information; or

    e. SCI.

Protective Security Service. A transportation protective service provided by a cleared commercial carrier qualified by the SDDC to transport SECRET shipments.

Reference Material. Documentary material over which the GCA, who lets the classified contract, does not have classification jurisdiction, and did not have classification jurisdiction at the time the material was originated. Most material made available to contractors by the DTIC and other secondary distribution agencies is reference material as thus defined.

Remote Terminal. A device for communication with an automated IS from a location that is not within the central computer facility.

Restricted Area. A controlled access area established to safeguard classified material, that because of its size or nature, cannot be adequately protected during working hours by the usual safeguards, but that is capable of being stored during non-working hours in an approved repository or secured by other methods approved by the CSA.

Restricted Data (RD). All data concerning the design, manufacture, or use of atomic weapons; the production of special nuclear material; or the use of special nuclear material in the production of energy, but shall not include data declassified or removed from the RD category pursuant to section 142 of reference (c).

SAP. Any program that is established to control access, distribution, and to provide protection for particularly sensitive classified information beyond that normally required for TOP SECRET, SECRET, or CONFIDENTIAL information. A SAP can be created or continued only as authorized by a senior agency official delegated such authority pursuant to reference (b).

SECRET. The classification level applied to information, the unauthorized disclosure of which reasonably could be expected to cause serious damage to the national security that the original classification authority is able to identify or describe.

Security in Depth. A determination made by the CSA that a contractor's security program consists of layered and complementary security controls sufficient to deter and detect unauthorized entry and movement within the facility.

Security Violation. Failure to comply with the policy and procedures established by this Manual that reasonably could result in the loss or compromise of classified information.

Shipper. One who releases custody of material to a carrier for transportation to a consignee. (See "Consignor.")

Source Document. A classified document, other than a classification guide, from which information is extracted for inclusion in another document.

Standard Practice Procedures (SPP). A document(s) prepared by a contractor that implements the applicable requirements of this Manual for the contractor's operations and involvement with classified information at the contractor's facility.

Subcontract. Any contract entered into by a contractor to furnish supplies or services for performance of a prime contract or a subcontract. For purposes of this Manual a subcontract is any contract, subcontract, purchase order, lease agreement, service agreement, request for quotation (RFQ), request for proposal (RFP), invitation for bid (IFB), or other agreement or procurement action between contractors that requires or will require access to classified information to fulfill the performance requirements of a prime contract.

Subcontractor. A supplier, distributor, vendor, or firm that furnishes supplies or services to or for a prime contractor or another subcontractor, who enters into a contract with a prime contractor. For purposes of this Manual, each subcontractor shall be considered as a prime contractor in relation to its subcontractors.

Subsidiary Corporation. A corporation in which another corporation owns at least a majority of its voting securities.

System Software. Computer programs that control, monitor, or facilitate use of the IS; for example, operating systems, programming languages, communication, input-output control, sorts, security packages and other utility-type programs. Considered to also include off-the-shelf application packages obtained from manufacturers and commercial vendors, such as for word processing, spreadsheets, data base management, graphics, and computer-aided design.

Technical Data. Information governed by reference (v) and the Export Administration Regulation (EAR) (reference (y)). The export of technical data that is inherently military in character is controlled by reference (v). The export of technical data that has both military and civilian uses is controlled by reference (y).

TOP SECRET. The classification level applied to information, the unauthorized disclosure of which reasonable could be expected to cause exceptionally grave damage to the national security that the original classification authority is able to identify or describe.

Transclassified Foreign Nuclear Information (TFNI). Defined in the DOE Order 475.2B (reference (as)).

Transmission. The sending of information from one place to another by radio, microwave, laser, or other nonconnective methods, as well as by cable, wire, or other connective medium. Transmission also includes movement involving the actual transfer of custody and responsibility for a document or other classified material from one authorized addressee to another.

Transshipping Activity. A government activity to which a carrier transfers custody of freight for reshipment by another carrier to the consignee.

UK Community. Consists of the UK Government entities with facilities and non-governmental facilities identified on the DDTC website (http://www.pmddtc.state.gov/) at the time of export.

Unauthorized Person. A person not authorized to have access to specific classified information in accordance with the requirements of this Manual.

United States. The 50 states and the District of Columbia.

United States and its Territorial Areas. The 50 states, the District of Columbia, Puerto Rico, Guam, American Samoa, the Virgin Islands, Wake Island, Johnston Atoll, Kingman Reef, Palmyra Atoll, Baker Island, Howland Island, Jarvis Island, Midway Islands, Navassa Island, and Northern Mariana Islands.

NOTE: From 18 July 1947 until 1 October 1994, the United States administered the Trust Territory of the Pacific Islands; it entered into a political relationship with all four political units: the Northern Mariana Islands is a commonwealth in political union with the United States (effective 3 November 1986); the Republic of the Marshall Islands signed a Compact of Free Association with United States (effective 21 October 1986); the Federated States of Micronesia signed a Compact of Free Association with the United States (effective 3 November 1986); Palau concluded a Compact of Free Association with the United States (effective 1 October 1994).

U.S. Person. Any form of business enterprise or entity organized, chartered or incorporated under the laws of the United States or its territories and any person who is a citizen or national of the United States.

Upgrade. A determination that certain classified information, in the interest of national security, requires a higher degree of protection against unauthorized disclosure than currently provided, coupled with a changing of the classification designation to reflect such a higher degree.

Voting Securities. Any securities that presently entitle the owner or holder thereof to vote for the election of directors of the issuer or, with respect to unincorporated entities, individuals exercising similar functions.

Working Hours. The period of time when:

a. There is present in the specific area where classified material is located, a work force on a regularly scheduled shift, as contrasted with employees

working within an area on an overtime basis outside of the scheduled work shift; and

b. The number of employees in the scheduled work force is sufficient in number and so positioned to be able to detect and challenge the presence of unauthorized personnel. This would, therefore, exclude janitors, maintenance personnel, and other individuals whose duties require movement throughout the facility.

Working Papers. Documents or materials, regardless of the media, which are expected to be revised prior to the preparation of a finished product for dissemination or retention.

APPENDIX D

NISPOM Supplement - Security Requirements for SAPs, SCI, IC Compartmented Programs, RD, and FRD

1. **General**. Given the sensitive nature of the classified information in these categories, the security requirements prescribed in this appendix are in addition to NISPOM standards, and must be applied through specific contract requirements.

    1.1. The contractor will comply with the security measures reflected in this appendix and other issuances specifically referenced, when applied by the GCA or designee as part of a contract. Acceptance of the contract security measures is a prerequisite to any negotiations leading to program participation and an area accreditation (e.g., a SCIF or a SAP facility accreditation).

    1.2. In some cases, security or sensitive factors of a CSA-created program may require security measures that exceed the standards of this appendix. In such cases, the CSA-imposed higher standards specifically detailed in the contract or conveyed through other applicable directives will be binding on government and contractor participants. In cases of doubt over the specific provisions, the contractor should consult the program security officer and the contracting officer before taking any action or expending program-related funds. In cases of extreme emergency requiring immediate attention, the action taken should protect the government's interest and the security of the program from compromise.

    1.3. Every effort will be made to avoid waivers to established standards unless they are in the best interest of the government. In those cases where waivers are deemed necessary, a request will be submitted in accordance with the procedures established by the CSA.

2. **SAPS**.

    2.1. **DoD SAP Contracts**. Contractors will implement the security requirements for SAPs codified in SAP-related policy, when established by contract, in accordance with applicable statutes, Executive orders, CSA directives, instructions, manuals, regulations, standards, memorandums, and other SAP security related policy documents.

    2.2. **Non-DoD SAPS.** Contractors performing on SAP contracts issued by other than DoD GCAs, will implement SAP protection requirements imposed in their contracts. These requirements may be from, but are not limited to, statutes, Executive orders, CSA directives, instructions, manuals, regulations, standards, memorandums, and other SAP security related policy documents.

3. **Alternative Compensatory Control Measures (ACCM).** Contractors may participate in ACCMs, or be directed to participate, only when such access and the associated security plan are identified in DD Form 254. Care must be taken to ensure identification of the security plan does not disclose ACCM-protected data.

    3.1. **ACCM Contracts.** DoD contractors will implement the security requirements for ACCMs, when established by contract, in accordance with applicable statutes, Executive orders, CSA directives, instructions, manuals, regulations, standards, memorandums, and other SAP security related policy documents.

    3.2. **Non-DoD with ACCMs.** Contractors performing on ACCM contracts issued by other than DoD GCAs, will implement ACCM protection requirements imposed in their contracts.

4. **IC Compartmented Programs**

    4.1. This section encompasses SCI and IC SAPs (collectively referred to in this issuance as "Controlled Access Programs (CAPs)") requiring compartmentation and enhanced protection when the vulnerability of, or threat to, specific information is exceptional and normal standards, criteria, processes, and accesses are insufficient to protect such information from unauthorized disclosure.

    4.2. Contractors will implement the security requirements for CAPs in accordance with applicable CAP-related issuances, when established by contract. These issuances include all DNI security-related policy documents that may pertain to the protection of CAP and CAP-related information.

5. RD, FRD, and TFNI

5.1. **General**. This section describes requirements for nuclear-related information designated RD, FRD, or TFNI in accordance with reference (c). Part 1045 of Title 10, CFR (reference (p)) contains the requirements for classification and declassification of RD and FRD. Additional handling and protection requirements are included in DOE policy.

5.1.1 Control and distribution of RD will be sufficient to assure common defense and security. Weapon data is always RD or FRD, specifically that portion concerning design, manufacture, or use of atomic weapons. RD and FRD categories are distinguished from the NSI category, which is governed in accordance with reference (b). It is necessary to differentiate between the handling of this information and NSI because of its direct relationship to our nation's nuclear deterrent.

5.1.2 Principal authority for setting requirements for classifying, accessing, handling, and securing and protecting RD is entrusted to the Secretary of Energy.

5.1.3 Some access requirements for RD and FRD exceed the requirements for NSI. It is important to note that due to the unique national security implications of RD and FRD, and to facilitate maintaining consistency of codified requirement, they are not repeated in the baseline NISPOM, but may be applied through specific contract requirements.

5.1.4 When RD is transclassified to TFNI, it is safeguarded as NSI. Such information will be labeled as TFNI. The label TFNI will be included on documents to indicate it is exempt from automatic declassification as specified in part 1045 of reference (p) and references (c), (b,) and (z).

5.2. **Unauthorized Disclosures**. Contractors will report all unauthorized disclosures involving RD, FRD and TFNI information to the CSA.

5.3. **International Requirements**. Reference (c) provides for a program of international cooperation to promote common defense and security and to make available to cooperating nations the benefits of peaceful applications of atomic energy as widely as expanding technology and considerations of the common defense and security will permit. Pursuant to section 123 of reference (c), information controlled by reference (c) may be shared with another nation only under the terms of an agreement for cooperation. The disclosure by a contractor of RD and FRD will not be permitted until an agreement is signed by the United States and participating governments, and disclosure guidance and security arrangements are established. RD and FRD will not be transmitted to a foreign national or regional defense organization unless such action is approved and undertaken under an agreement for cooperation between the U.S. and the cooperating entity and supporting statutory determinations, as prescribed in reference (c).

5.4. **Personnel Security Clearances and Access**. Only DOE, NRC, DoD, and NASA can grant access to RD and FRD that is under their cognizance. Access to RD and FRD must be granted in accordance with reference(c). Baseline requirements for access to RD and FRD are codified in specific DoD, DOE, NRC, and NASA directives and regulations. In addition, need-to-know and other restrictions on access may apply.

5.5. **Classification and Declassification**

5.5.1 All persons with access to RD and FRD must be trained on the authorities required to classify and declassify RD and FRD information and documents and on handling procedures in accordance with parts 1045 and 1016 of reference (p).

5.5.2 Any person who believes he or she has information that may be RD or FRD must submit it to an RD classifier for evaluation.

5.5.3 Only RD classifiers may classify documents containing RD or FRD. RD classifiers must be trained on the procedures for classifying, declassifying, marking, and handling RD, or FRD and documents in accordance with part 1045 of reference (p).

5.5.4 RD classifiers will use classification guides as the primary basis for classifying documents containing RD, FRD, and TFNI.

5.5.5. RD classifiers cannot declassify a document marked as containing RD, FRD, or TFNI. Declassification includes redacting RD, FRD, and

TFNI portions from a document and removing RD, FRD, and TFNI markings from documents. RD documents must be sent to designated individuals in DOE. FRD documents must be sent to designated individuals in DOE or appropriate officials in DoD.

5.5.6 RD and FRD documents must include:

5.5.6.1 The RD classifier's name and position or title.

5.5.6.2 The classification guide or source document (by title and date) used to classify the document.

5.5.7 No date or event for automatic declassification ever applies to RD, FRD or TFNI documents, even if they contain classified NSI. RD, FRD or TFNI documents remain classified until a positive action by a designated DOE official (for RD, FRD or TFNI) or an appropriate DoD official (for FRD) is taken to declassify them.

5.5.8 Any RD or FRD document intended for public release in an RD or FRD subject area must be reviewed for classification by the appropriate DOE organization (for RD or TFNI) or the appropriate DOE or DoD organization (for FRD) prior to its release.

5.5.9 Consult DOE Manual 205.1B (reference (at)) for additional information and requirements. Contact the DOE Office of Classification at outreach@hq.doe.gov or at (301) 903-7567 for additional information concerning the classification and declassification of RD and FRD.

5.6. **Automatic declassification**. Documents containing TFNI are excluded from the automatic declassification provisions of part 1045 of reference (p) until the TFNI designation is properly removed by DOE. When DOE determines that a TFNI designation may be removed, any remaining information classified must be referred to the appropriate agency in accordance with reference (c) and part 1045 of reference (p).

5.7. **Challenges to RD, FRD and TFNI Classification**. Any contractor employee who believes that an RD, FRD, or TFNI document is classified improperly or unnecessarily may challenge that classification following the procedures established by the GCA.

5.8. **Comingling**. Comingling of RD, FRD, and TFNI with information classified, in accordance with reference (b), in the same document should be avoided to the greatest degree possible. When mixing this information cannot be avoided, the protection requirements of references (b) and (z), as well as Part 2003 of reference (z) must be met.

5.9. **Marking RD and FRD**. RD and FRD, in addition to any traditional NSI classification markings, will include RD category admonishment information on the first page, RD or FRD marked at the top and bottom of each interior page containing it, and notation of Sigma information. These markings may appear on any classification level (CONFIDENTIAL, SECRET, or TOP SECRET) documents. Weapon data documents being sent outside the weapons complex will bear the marking NUCLEAR WEAPON DATA, or CNWDI, as appropriate. Further information regarding these requirements can be found at https://www.directives.doe.gov/ and www.nnsa.energy.gov or, by e-mail to Security.Directives@hq.doe.gov.

5.10. **Protection of RD and FRD**. Most of the protection requirements for RD and FRD are similar to NSI and are based on the classification level; however, there are some specific protection requirements for certain Sigma information that may be applied through specific contract requirements by the GCA. These range from distribution limitations through the limitation of access to specifically authorized individuals to specific storage requirements, including the requirement for intrusion detection systems, and additional accountability records (i.e., Sigmas 14, 15, and 20).

5.10.1 Any DOE contractor that violates a classified information security requirement may be subject to a civil penalty under the provisions of part 824 of reference (p).

5.10.2 Certification is required for individuals authorized access to specific Sigmas, as appropriate. Address questions regarding these requirements to Security.Directives@hq.doe.gov.

5.10.3 Storage and distribution requirements are determined by the classification level, category, and Sigma. All RD documents do not require a Sigma designation. Storage and distribution requirements will be dependent only on classification level and category.

5.11. **Accountability**. In addition to TS information, some S/RD information is considered accountable (e.g., specific Sigma 14, 15, and 20 documents.) Each weapon data control point will keep a record of transactions involving Secret weapon data documents under its jurisdiction including origination, receipt, transmission, current custodian, reproduction, change of classification, declassification, and destruction.

5.12. **Cyber**. Classified databases, systems and networks containing RD and FRD are protected under the requirements developed and distributed by the DOE Office of the Chief Information Officer.

5.13. **References**. The following may not have been previously referenced, but are some of the primary directives that cover RD and FRD. Information regarding copies of DOE Security Directives may be requested via e-mail at: Security.Directives@hq.doe.gov.

5.13.1 **Reference (at)**. Reference (at) provides baseline requirements and controls for the graded protection of the confidentiality, integrity, and availability of classified information and IS used or operated by the DOE, contractors, and any other organization on behalf of DOE, including the National Nuclear Security Administration.

5.13.2 **DOE Order 452.7 (Reference (au))**. Reference (au) establishes a general process and provides direction for controlling access to and distributing Sigma 14 and 15 nuclear weapon data at the DOE. It supplements DOE Order 452.4B (reference (av)), which establishes DOE requirements and responsibilities to prevent the deliberate unauthorized use of U.S. nuclear explosives and nuclear weapons.

5.13.3 **DOE Order 473.3 (Reference (aw))**. Reference (aw) establishes requirements for the physical protection of safeguards and security interests. Copies of certain sections of reference (aw) (e.g., Attachment 3, Annex 1, Safeguards and Security Alarm Management System, which contains Unclassified Controlled Nuclear Information) are only available, by request, from Security.Directives@hq.doe.gov or, by phone at (301) 903-1159.

5.13.4 **DOE Order 471.6 (Reference (ax))**. Reference (ax) establishes security requirements for the protection and control of matter required to be classified or controlled by statutes, regulations, or DOE directives.

5.13.5 **DOE Order 483.1-1A (Reference ay)**. Reference (ay) provides policy, requirements, and responsibilities for the oversight, management and administration of Cooperative Research and Development Agreement activities at DOE facilities.

About Red Bike Publishing

For more information on NISPOM, books, training and security, see our video @ www.redbikepublishing.com/security

Our company is registered as a government contractor company with the CCR and VetBiz (DUNS 826859691). Red Bike Publishing provides high quality books and include the following which can be found at www.redbikepublishing.com and Amazon.com:

PUBLISHING
Get Rich in a Niche-The Insider's Guide to Self-Publishing in a Specialized
Industry ISBN: 978-1-936800-04-9

OTHER TOPICS

1. Rainy Street Stories-Reflections on Secret Wars, Espionage and Terrorism
ISBN: 978-1-936800-10-0
2. 2000 Miles On Wisdom ISBN: 978-1-936800-20-9
3. Next In Line Please ISBN: 978-1-936800-15-5

NOVELS
Commitment-A Novel ASIN: B0057U3GLS
Devoted ASIN: B015HTZW1K

NATIONAL SECURITY TOPICS

1. DoD Security Clearances and Contracts Guidebook ISBN 978-1- 936800-80-3 and
ISBN 978-1-936800-99-5
2. Insider's Guide to Security Clearances ISBN: 9781936800988
3. ISP Certification-The Industrial Security Professional Exam
Manual ISBN: 9780981620602
4. National Industrial Security Program Operating Manual (NISPOM) ISBN: 978098162060857
5. International Traffic in Arms Regulation (ITAR) ISBN: 97809816288

ARMY TOPICS

1. Ranger Handbook SH 21-76 ISBN-13: 978-1936800087
2. US Army Physical Readiness Training TC 3.22-20 ISBN:97809816240
3. US Army Physical Fitness Training FM 21-20 ISBN:97809816240
4. US Army Leadership FM 6-22 ISBN: 978-0981620671
5. US Army Drill and Ceremonies FM 3-21.5 ISBN: 978-1936800025

A special word of thanks and a favor to ask

Thank you for ordering our print version of NISPOM. I really hope you find it helpful.

I really would really love to hear your feedback and your input would help to make the next version of this book and my future books better.

Please leave me a helpful review on Amazon letting me know what you thought of the book.

Thanks so much and best of success to you!!
Jeffrey W. Bennett.
editor@redbikepublishing.
www.redbikepublishing.com

We have a gift for you. Check out a NISPOM Training presentation and a video.

http://www.redbikepublishing.com/security/

CPSIA information can be obtained
at www.ICGtesting.com
Printed in the USA
LVHW061644030722
722680LV00006B/85